· Pt out list of Aghamore townlands
for townland search

- Chapel of Ease - look for
- seems a chapel pl
& admin. by another

- Tithe Aghamore 1833
- Linen / Flax Grower 1796 — no Flanagan Mayo
Owen Rooney Creggan
Francis Roony Armagh
Patrick Loy
Owen Loy Creggan
- 179C Catholics migrating from Ulster to Mayo
2 Morongs in Kilfarboy

A GUIDE TO TRACING YOUR MAYO ANCESTORS

- 1830/31 Voters of Mayo
- 1832-9 Mayo Freeholders

Ordnance Survey Field Name Book
- Civil Parish of Aughamore (Aghamore, aH. Agharower)

Samuel Lewis (description & maps)
Samuel Lewis

Note: Most of the post-1870 church marriage records list the mother's name

A Guide to Tracing your Mayo Ancestors

Brian Smith

FLYLEAF PRESS

First published in 1997 by
Flyleaf Press
4 Spencer Villas
Glenageary
Co. Dublin
Ireland
Ph (01) 2806228

British Library cataloguing in Publication Data available

ISBN 0 9508466 7 8

Cover design by Cathy Henderson showing Rockfleet Castle, principal residence of Grace O'Malley

Dedication

To the memory of my nephew

Robert Kelly

1975-1993

Acknowledgements

I wish to express my gratitude for the valuable assistance afforded to me by the staff of the following Dublin repositories:

The National Library of Ireland
The National Archives of Ireland
The Registry of Deeds
General Register Office
The Gilbert Library
Dun Laoghaire Central Library
Representative Church Body Library

and the Public Record Office of Northern Ireland, Belfast

My special thanks also to the following who provided information or other assistance:
Frieda Carroll, Archivist, Dun Laoghaire Genealogical Society
Sean Magee, Dun Laoghaire Genealogical Society
John and Martin Lyons of Aghamore and Dun Laoghaire
Joe Byrne of Aghamore
Ivor Hamrock, Mayo County Library
Gerard Delaney, South Mayo Family History Research Centre
Fiona Lynn Forde, Mayo North Family History Research Centre
Bronagh Joyce, Westport Historical Society
Carmel Hughes, North Mayo Historical and Archaeological Society
Robert H. Bonar, Presbyterian Historical Society of Ireland
Rev. Ian D. Henderson, Methodist Church, Sligo
Desiree Breslin, for the endless typing

To all my family for their encouragement and assistance.

· What about
- evictions
- emigration (land owner-paid / self-paid)
- famine
- poor houses

Table of Contents

	Abbreviations	9
Chapter 1.	Introduction	11
Chapter 2.	How to use this Book	13
Chapter 3.	Administrative Divisions	15
Chapter 4.	Civil Registration	25
Chapter 5.	Censuses, Census Substitutes and Other Sources	29
Chapter 6.	Church Records	41
Chapter 7.	Wills, Administrations and Marriage Licences	51
Chapter 8.	Land Records	57
Chapter 9.	Directories	63
Chapter10.	Newspapers	65
Chapter 11.	Surnames, Family Histories & Related Papers	69
Chapter 12.	Gravestone Inscriptions	73
Chapter 13.	Mayo in 1798	77
Chapter 14.	Further Reading	79
Chapter 15.	Addresses	83
	Index	89
	Index to Illustrations	95

Abbreviations Used

Arch.	Archaeological
b.	birth/born
bapt.	Baptism
BELB	Belfast Education & Library Board
BL	British Library
Bo.	Barony
Burl.	Burial
Co.	County
CoI	Church of Ireland
CDB	Congested Districts Board
d.	death/died
DKPRI	(Reports of the)Deputy Keeper of Public Records of Ireland
GO	Genealogical Office
GRO	General Register Office
Hist.	Historical
ILC	Irish Land Commission
IMC	Irish Manuscripts Commission
Ir. Gen.	Irish Genealogist
JAPMD	Journal of the Association of the Preservation of the Memorials of the Dead in Ireland.
J. or Jnl.	Journal
RSAI	Journal of Royal Society of Antiquarians of Ireland
LC	Local Custody
m. or marr.	marriage/married
MCL	Mayo County Library
mf.	microfilm
MNFHRC	Mayo North Family History Research Centre
Ms/Mss	Manuscript/s
NAI	National Archives of Ireland (formerly PRO)
NLI	National Library of Ireland
OP	Official Papers
PHSI	Presbyterian Historical Society of Ireland

Pos.	Positive
PRONI	Public Record Office of Northern Ireland
Pub.	published/publisher
RCBL	Representative Church Body Library
RIA	Royal Irish Academy
RSAI	Royal Society of Antiquarians in Ireland
SLC	Family History Library, Salt Lake City (& branches)
SMFHRC	South Mayo Family History Research Centre (see p xx)
Soc.	Society
SOG	Society of Genealogists, London
TCD	Trinity College Dublin

Chapter 1 Introduction

Mayo is situated on the Northwest coast of Ireland and is the second largest county in the province of Connaught, covering an area of 1.3 million acres. It extends from 53°28' to 54°21' north latitude and from 8°25' to 10°5' west longitude. The county adjoins County Galway on the South and this border is partly formed by Lough Corrib and the long narrow fjord of Killary Harbour. It is bounded on the West and North by the Atlantic ocean and by the counties of Sligo and Roscommon on the east.

The landscape varies from relatively flat land in East Mayo, through large island-studded lakes, like Lough Conn, Lough Carra, Lough Mask, to the naked quartzite peaks along the Atlantic coast. This coast has both rugged cliffs and sandy beaches. North Mayo has extensive tracts of blanket bog, and some good agricultural land, while South Mayo is more mountainous. It is a county with many scenic landscapes, and a rich archaeological and historical heritage. It is therefore a popular tourism county with amenities of interest to the naturalist, (family) historian, and sportsman alike.Although picturesque, the land is mainly poor and much of the land is bog or mountain. The current population is 111,500 and the major towns are Castlebar, Crossmolina, Ballinrobe, Ballina, Killala and Westport.

Although Mayo was probably first inhabited around 7000 BC, the earliest evidence is from the fourth millennium BC. In this, the Neolithic, period, the first farmers arrived, and introduced agriculture and animal husbandry as well as the skills of pottery-making and weaving. Around 160 megalithic tombs built by these people, the earliest surviving architectural structures in the country, are in Mayo. As this is over 10% of the total number of such tombs found in all of Ireland, the Mayo region was clearly of importance during the Neolithic period. It retained this importance into the Bronze Age (c. 2000- 400 BC) when this phase of tomb-building came to an end.

The blanket bog which covered parts of Ireland from the late 3rd millennium BC onwards also covered, in some places, the field systems, habitation-sites and tombs of these early farmers. Extensive pre-bog field-systems with stone walls have been discovered embedded in the bog in many parts of Ireland. The Behy/Glenulra region, west of Ballycastle in County Mayo, contains a 1,500 hectare archaeological site of this type, known as the 'Céide Fields'. This is the most extensive Stone Age monument in the world.

County Mayo got its name from a diocese of that name which evolved from a 7th century monastery of Maigh Eo established by Saint Colmán. The Irish name Maigh Eo, meaning 'plain of yew-trees' was later anglicised to Mayo. When the county was established by the English around 1570, it was called 'Mayo'after this monastery and diocese.

Further details on Mayo, including amenities and a history of Mayo (by Bernard O'Hara and Nollaig O'Muraíle) is available on the Internet at http://www.mayo-ireland.ie/MotM.htm

The families of county Mayo are a mix of native Gaelic families, Norman families and immigrant Gaelic families from Northern Ireland and a small number of other immigrants from various places. The major original Gaelic inhabitants included the families of Gallagher, Kelly, Moran, O'Malley and Duffy (see page X). From the 12th century, there was also Norman occupation of the county, in particular by the families of Burke, Barrett and Walsh.

During the 16th century the sectarian struggle in Northern Ireland resulted in the enforced migration of many thousands of Catholics from Ulster counties to Mayo. These migrants were settled as tenants on several of the major estates in the county.

The county was predominantly involved in agriculture and fisheries and had few industries. In 1798 the Irish rebelled against English rule, and Mayo became the battleground for one of the major events of that war. The French General Humbert, and 11,000 men landed at Killala to assist the Irish rebels. This army was defeated after a brief campaign and significant imprisonment and land confiscations in the county resulted. These events, and the records which exist, are detailed in chapter 13.

The county was significantly affected by the Great Famine of 1845-47 which resulted in the death or emigration of 30% of the population by 1851.

Mayo has 2 Heritage centres in which the family records of the county are being indexed (see p 84), and also several active local history societies.

The author, Brian Smith, also conducts research on Mayo families. He can be contacted at 48 Clarinda Park East, Dun Laoghaire, Co. Dublin, Ireland.

Chapter 2 How to Use This Book

Tracing a family history normally requires the researcher to consult many different historical sources, in some (or hopefully all) of which details of the family may be found. Sufficient details, when pieced together, can form a comprehensive picture of a family's existence. The final picture depends on the number and quality of these details. Mayo, like many other Western Irish counties, does not have a rich store of records. It is therefore important to know the full range of available sources, and to use them effectively. These sources vary widely in their genealogical content and can be described as either Primary Sources (e.g. civil registration of births, marriages and deaths, church records, census records and wills and administrations) or Secondary Sources (i.e. records that assist the researcher to locate the existence in an area at a particular time, e.g. land records). Some of the above will also provide the researcher with interesting background details.

Other sources can also be of great assistance in providing information about the life style of an ancestor. They can in some cases be used to define a time frame in which a primary source can be consulted. They include newspapers, journal articles and published family histories and documents.

There is no magic formula for successful research. However, initial research should be based on the following principles:

(a) Record as much detail as possible from living relatives. Even dubious information from this source should not be ignored until the true facts are established. Elimination is as much a part of genealogy as confirmation.

(b) Construct a pedigree chart so as not to confuse different generations, especially when one personal (Christian) name is very common within a family, as is often the case.

(c) Work from the known to the unknown, i.e. always try to establish a connection between a known family member and a previous generation, or another potential family member. Many Irish family names are locally common and it is easy to presume a connection that is not real.

Having gathered as much detail as possible from your family members and papers, you should plan to verify and expand this information using the available records. This book is designed to help you do this. The nature, time-frames and locations of the available sources are described in the following chapters. Descriptions of available sources are arranged by chapter according to source type i.e. civil registration, church records, censuses, census substitutes, newspapers, directories etc.

For optimal use of these records, it is important to understand the system of administrative divisions used in Ireland. These divisions or areas are described in Chapter 3. They are vital in determining an ancestor's address or location. Many, if not most, sources are arranged according to such divisions, and an understanding of the different elements of an ancestors address is therefore important.

The abbreviations used are explained on p. 9, and contact details for the organisations and archives cited are in Chap. 15. Most publications cited are to be found in major genealogical libraries.

While County Mayo is not as wealthy in genealogical sources as some other counties, the collection of primary, secondary and other sources covered will help provide the researcher with a fascinating insight as to how and where an ancestor lived.

Chapter 3 Administrative Divisions

County Mayo was, and is, divided into different units or divisions for the purposes of both Civil and Ecclesiastical administration. In short, the state and the church divided the county into geographical units which suited their particular purposes. These divisions are an important factor in locating the records mentioned throughout this book. The divisions the researcher will come across are as follows:

Civil Divisions

Townland

The townland is the smallest civil division within a county. It is an ancient division of land which is highly variable in size, and may vary from less than 10 acres to several thousand. It is the most specific part of an ancestors address in rural areas.

Civil Parish

The civil parish is the land division which most commonly occurs in Irish records. There are 73 civil parishes in Mayo, and each is formed of many townlands. (See map p. 24.)
It should be noted that some civil parishes cross barony and county boundaries. In some cases also, civil parishes are divided into unconnected parts. For instance, Kilcolman parish is partly in the barony of Clanmorris and partly in the barony of Costello. Likewise the parish of Kilcommon can be found in the northern barony of Erris and in the southern barony of Kilmaine.

Barony

Civil parishes are grouped into Baronies. This division is generally based on the ancient 'tuath' or territory of an Irish clan. There are 9 baronies in Co. Mayo but they are not as widely used in records as the civil parishes. The baronies of Mayo are: Burrishoole, Carra, Clanmorris, Costello, Erris, Gallen, Kilmaine, Murrisk and Tyrawley. See map p. 24.

Poor Law Union

These were established under the Poor Law Act of 1838 for use in the administration of distress relief and the upkeep of the poor and destitute. They are unrelated to any other division and do not adhere to county and barony borders. Each is based around (and named from) a major town in which was based the workhouse and other administrative functions of the Poor Law. The Poor Law Union (PLU) later came to be used as the area, or district, in which Civil Registration of births, marriages and deaths was conducted. There are 9

304 CENSUS OF IRELAND FOR THE YEAR 1851.

No. of Sheet of the Ordnance Survey Maps.	Townlands and Towns.	Area in Statute Acres.			County.	Barony.	Parish.	Poor Law Union in 1857.	Townland Census of 1851, Part I.	
		A.	R.	P.					Vol.	Page
28	Corglass . . .	126	0	27a	Cavan . .	Clankee . . .	Bailieborough . .	Bailieborough .	III.	71
29, 35	Corglass . . .	193	2	29	Cavan . .	Clankee . . .	Enniskeen . .	Bailieborough .	III.	72
31	Corglass . . .	290	3	8b	Cavan . .	Clanmahon . .	Crosserlough . .	Cavan . .	III.	76
19, 20	Corglass . . .	221	3	9c	Cavan . .	Lower Loughtee .	Drumlane . .	Cavan . .	III.	79
21, 22	Corglass . . .	58	2	24	Cavan . .	Tullygarvey . .	Drung . . .	Cootehill . .	III.	88
25	Corglass . . .	74	0	3	Cavan . .	Upper Loughtee .	Annagelliff . .	Cavan . .	III.	81
32	Corglass . . .	142	3	37	Cavan . .	Upper Loughtee .	Denn . . .	Cavan . .	III.	83
30	Corglass . . .	423	0	22d	Leitrim . .	Carrigallen . .	Carrigallen . .	Bawnboy . .	IV.	89
18	Corglass . . .	141	0	7e	Leitrim . .	Drumahaire . .	Drumreilly . .	Carᵏ.on Shannon	IV.	95
20	Corglass . . .	36	3	29	Leitrim . .	Drumahaire . .	Inishmagrath . .	Manorhamilton	IV.	96
24	Corglass . . .	134	2	12f	Leitrim . .	Leitrim . . .	Kiltubbrid . .	Carᵏ. on Shannon	IV.	103
3, 6	Corglass . . .	1,034	0	2g	Leitrim . .	Rosclogher . .	Killasnet . .	Manorhamilton	IV.	109
2	Corglass . . .	750	0	0h	Longford . .	Longford . .	Killoe . . .	Longford . .	I.	156
18	Corglass . . .	87	2	35	Monaghan .	Dartree . . .	Ematris . . .	Cootehill . .	III.	266
4	Corglass . . .	287	0	9	Roscommon .	Boyle . . .	Kilronan . . .	Boyle . .	IV.	196
9	Corglass or Agha-nergill . . .	93	0	1	Armagh . .	Oneilland West .	Drumcree . .	Lurgan . .	III.	51
22, 25	Corglass or Cloverhill	97	3	26	Leitrim . .	Carrigallen . .	Oughteragh . .	Bawnboy . .	IV.	92
38	Corglass or Rassan .	96	0	35	Cavan . .	Castlerahan . .	Crosserlough . .	Oldcastle . .	III.	68
25	Corgloghan . .	90	0	8	Leitrim . .	Carrigallen . .	Drumreilly . .	Bawnboy . .	IV.	90
2	Corgorman . .	160	1	18	Roscommon .	Boyle . . .	Kilronan . . .	Boyle . .	IV.	196
23	Corgowan . .	172	2	34	Roscommon .	Ballintober North .	Kilglass . . .	Strokestown .	IV.	186
10, 11	Corgreagh . .	64	0	26i	Cavan . .	Lower Loughtee .	Drumlane . .	Cavan . .	III.	79
22	Corgreagh . .	243	3	2	Cavan . .	Tullygarvey . .	Kildrumsherdan .	Cootehill . .	III.	90
21	Corgreagh . .	138	0	15	Cavan . .	Upper Loughtee .	Larah . . .	Cavan . .	III.	85
26, 27	Corgreagh . .	378	2	25	Monaghan .	Cremorne . .	Aghnamullen . .	Carrickmacross	III.	257
1, 2	Corgreagh or Killagriff	412	3	17	Meath . .	Lower Kells . .	Moybolgue . .	Kells . .	I.	203
1	Corgreenan . .	59	0	0	Monaghan .	Trough . . .	Errigal Trough .	Clogher . .	III.	263
10	Corgrig . . .	357	0	11	Limerick . .	Shanid . . .	Robertstown . .	Glin . . .	II.	257
11	Corgullion . .	227	2	19	Roscommon .	Ballintober North .	Kilmore . . .	Carᵏ.on Shannon	IV.	187
17	Corhammock . .	324	0	35	Armagh . .	Fews Lower . .	Kilclooney . .	Armagh . .	III.	46
24	Corhanagh . .	359	0	38	Cavan . .	Tullyhunco . .	Killashandra . .	Cavan . .	III.	97
27	Corhawnagh . .	68	2	17	Leitrim . .	Leitrim . . .	Kiltoghert . .	Carᵏ. on Shannon	IV.	101
81	Corhawnagh . .	189	1	36	Mayo . .	Costello . . .	Aghamore . .	Swineford . .	IV.	137
20	Corhawnagh . .	516	2	7	Sligo . .	Leyny . . .	Ballysadare . .	Sligo . .	IV.	230
29	Corhawny . .	157	2	11	Roscommon .	Roscommon . .	Lissonuffy . .	Strokestown .	IV.	211
27	Corhelshinagh .	297	0	0j	Monaghan .	Cremorne . .	Aghnamullen . .	Carrickmacross	III.	257
33	Corhober . .	120	1	14	Sligo . .	Corran . . .	Emlaghfad . .	Sligo . .	IV.	226
8, 12	Corhollan . .	125	3	7k	Monaghan .	Monaghan . .	Drumsnat . .	Monaghan . .	III.	275
25, 26	Corhoogan . .	62	3	31	Cavan . .	Upper Loughtee .	Annagelliff . .	Cavan . .	III.	81
17	Corick . . .	181	1	21	Cavan . .	Tullygarvey . .	Kildrumsherdan .	Cootehill . .	III.	90
31	Corick . . .	1,133	0	27	Londonderry .	Keenaght . .	Dungiven . .	NewTⁿ.Limavady	III.	236
40, 45	Corick . . .	1,181	1	36	Londonderry .	Loughinsholin . .	Ballynascreen . .	Magherafelt .	III.	239
58, 59	Corick . . .	219	3	16	Tyrone . .	Clogher . . .	Clogher . . .	Clogher . .	III.	292
18	Corickmore . .	249	3	24l	Tyrone . .	Strabane Upper .	Bodoney Upper .	Gortin . .	III.	324
28	Coriltaun . .	230	0	28m	Galway . .	Clare . . .	Donaghpatrick .	Tuam . .	IV.	19
22, 29	Corimla North .	333	0	23	Sligo . .	Tireragh . . .	Kilmoremoy . .	Ballina . .	IV.	235
22, 29	Corimla South .	967	0	34	Sligo . .	Tireragh . . .	Kilmoremoy . .	Ballina . .	IV.	235
46	Corkaboy . .	154	2	9	Kerry . .	Trughanacmy . .	Kilgarrylander .	Tralee . .	II.	210
21	Corkagh . . .	84	2	13	Dublin . .	Uppercross . .	Clondalkin . .	Dublin South .	I.	39
12, 13	Corkagh Beg . .	253	1	20	Sligo . .	Tireragh . . .	Templeboy . .	Dromore West .	IV.	236
21	Corkagh Demesne .	219	3	1	Dublin . .	Uppercross . .	Clondalkin . .	Dublin South .	I.	39
12	Corkagh More .	300	3	10	Sligo . .	Tireragh . . .	Templeboy . .	Dromore West .	IV.	236
17	Corkan . . .	352	1	37	Westmeath .	Rathconrath . .	Rathconrath . .	Mullingar .	I.	284
51	Corkanaknockaun .	61	1	3	Clare . .	Bunratty Lower .	Kilnasoolagh . .	Ennis . .	II.	6
71	Corkan Isle . .	101	0	14	Donegal . .	Raphoe . . .	Clonleigh . .	Strabane . .	III.	134
5	Corkanree . .	124	2	32	Limerick . .	Pubblebrien . .	St. Michaels . .	Limerick . .	II.	254
27	Corkashybane . .	258	1	15	Monaghan .	Farney . . .	Magheross . .	Carrickmacross	III.	273
27	Corkashyduff . .	146	2	16	Monaghan .	Farney . . .	Magheross . .	Carrickmacross	III.	273
87, 88	Corkbeg . . .	359	3	26	Cork, E.R. .	Imokilly . . .	Corkbeg . . .	Middleton .	II.	86
23	Corkeenagh . .	71	2	29n	Roscommon .	Roscommon . .	Clooncraff . .	Strokestown .	IV.	208
23	Corkeeran . .	214	2	18o	Monaghan .	Cremorne . .	Aghnamullen . .	Cootehill . .	III.	257
19	Corkeeran . .	211	0	26	Monaghan .	Cremorne . .	Ballybay . . .	Castleblayney .	III.	259
18, 23	Corkeeran . .	162	0	17	Monaghan .	Dartree . . .	Ematris . . .	Cootehill . .	III.	266
17	Corkeeran . .	117	0	30	Monaghan .	Dartree . . .	Killeevan . .	Clones . .	III.	267
31, 34	Corkeeran . .	147	1	1	Monaghan .	Farney . . .	Magheracloone .	Carrickmacross	III.	272
113, 114, 122, 123	Corker . . .	460	0	21	Galway . .	Kiltartan . .	Kiltartan . .	Gort . .	IV.	45
28	Corker . . .	141	2	5	Roscommon .	Roscommon . .	Kilcooley . .	Strokestown .	IV.	210
9	Corkeragh . .	199	3	13	Kildare . .	Clane . . .	Ballynafagh . .	Naas . .	I.	53
92	Corker Beg . .	201	0	25	Donegal . .	Banagh . . .	Killaghtee . .	Donegal . .	III.	109
35	Corkermain . .	382	1	2	Antrim . .	Upper Glenarm .	Carncastle . .	Larne . .	III.	24
83, 92	Corker More . .	759	1	31	Donegal . .	Banagh . . .	Killaghtee . .	Donegal . .	III.	109

(a) Including 5A. 0R. 1P. water.
(b) Including 45A. 0R. 12P. water.
(c) Including 79A. 3R. 22P. water.
(d) Including 8A. 0R. 30P. water.
(e) Including 5A. 1R. 0P. water.
(f) Including 26A. 2R. 8P. water.
(g) Including 17A. 1R. 8P. water.
(h) Including 40A. 2R. 0P. water.
(i) Including 1A. 2R. 21P. water.
(j) Including 62A. 2R. 28P. water.
(k) Including 6A. 1R. 8P. water.
(l) Including 7A. 0R. 18P. water.
(m) Including 27A. 0R. 29P. water.
(n) Including 3A. 2R. 0P. water.
(o) Including 19A. 0R. 31P. water.

A page from the General Alphabetical Index of the townlands and towns, parishes and baronies of Ireland (Thom's Dublin 1861)

PLU's in Mayo. See page xx

District Electoral Divisions

The District Electoral Division (DED) is a sub-division of the Poor Law union, in which census information was compiled and in which the census returns are also arranged. They were also used for the elections of local and national representatives established under the Local Government Act of 1898.

Ecclesiastical Divisions

Church of Ireland Parish

The ecclesiastical divisions used by the Church of Ireland (CoI) had a specific significance for record purposes as the CoI was also the 'Established' or State church. In this capacity it once performed several functions now performed by the State. These include Probate (proving of wills), and granting of marriage and other forms of licence. Church of Ireland divisions therefore have a relevance when researching certain record types.

While generally conforming to the civil parish boundaries, some CoI churches may have served several civil parishes. This is particularly so in Mayo where the CoI community was always small. Indeed, several civil parishes had no Church of Ireland church.

Catholic Church Parish

Catholic Church parishes boundaries rarely conform to those of the Civil parish, even though they may have the same name as the civil parish in which they are located. They are often of ancient origin, and generally larger in size than CoI parishes. Some areas have a Chapel of Ease which comes under the administration of the parish priest of an adjoining parish.

Useful Guides to Administrative Divisions

To establish the divisions which make up an ancestor's ìgenealogical addressî the following references are useful:

1851. Townland Index of Ireland:

This provides a full alphabetic listing of all of the Townlands, Towns, Civil Parishes and Baronies of Ireland giving their relative location, area and map reference. For each townland the relevant County, Barony, Civil Parish and Poor Law Union is provided.This listing was derived from the areas used by officials in collecting the 1851 Census. It was originally published by Thom's as 'An Index to the Townlands and Towns, Parishes and Baronies of Ireland '. It has been republished by the Genealogical Publishing Co., Baltimore, US and is widely available in libraries.

Similar volumes were compiled for the Censuses of 1841, 1861,1871 etc. and may be found in many libraries. The spelling and occurrence of some townlands varied between censuses and it may occasionally be useful to consult some of these.

Those conducting research on 17th century records may also be interested in the '1655-59 Index of Parishes & Townlands of Ireland'. This was compiled and edited by Yann Goblet, based on areas mentioned in Sir William Petty's Mss Barony Maps, and published

266

Aughamore (contd.)

The property of Domk. O'Reilly, Kildegan Castle Co. Kildare. It contains 436 a. 2 r. 26 p. Statute Measure including about 27 acres of Bog. There is an ancient Fort in this Townland, also a church, church ruins, and grave yard about the N.W. part of the Townland, and a Road passing thro' the central part of it from E. to W.

Curhaunagh 27

COR ṪAṀNAĊ, odd-field.

Curhawnagh -- T.O'C.
o?

Corhawnagh -- J.O'D.
o Curhaunagh

In the S.W. side of the Parish. Bounded on the S. by Ballinacostello and the Parish of Knock, E. by Melltran and on the N. and E. by Lissmaganshan and Lissmeagan Townlands. Sheet 81.

The property of Mr. James Beatagh, Maneen. It contains 189 a. 1 r. 36 p. Statute measure including about 63 acres of Bog. There is a Trigl. Station in the N. end of this Townland called Cashacor.

Lissmeegan -- T.O'C. 28
aun?
LIOS MÍOGAIN, Magan's fort.

Lismeegaun -- J.O'D.
Lismeagan -- Boundy. S. Sketch
o Lismagawn
Lismeegawn
Lismmigane -- Balls Map of Co. Mayo
Lishmigan -- Strafford's Survey of Co. Mayo

In a S. interior part of the Parish. Bounded on the N. & E. by Doogerra, on the S.E. and S. by Mountain in Common, Tubber and Ballinacostello, on the W. and N.W. by Curhaunagh and Lissmaganshon Townlands. Sheet 81.

The property of Mr. Beatagh, Maneen. It contains 25 a. 0 r. 20. p. Statute Measure including 148 acres of Bog or thereabouts, there is an ancient Fort in the S. end of this Townland.

A page from the Ordnance Survey Field Name Book for the Civil Parish of Aghamore (1838)

by the Irish Manuscripts Commission (Dublin 1932) NLI Ir. 9141 gb.

Lewis's Topographical Dictionary of Ireland (1837)

This 3-volume set contains an alphabetically arranged account of all civil parishes, major market towns, seaports and many villages. For each it provides a brief account of local history, social and economic conditions and major landowners (see Fig X). Both Catholic and non-Catholic divisions and churches are also described. A set of 32 county maps accompany this publication. The set has been republished by Kenny's of Galway, and also by Genealogical Publishing Co., Baltimore, US and is widely available in libraries. The maps are also republished in Donal F. Begley's, 'Handbook on Irish Genealogy' (Heraldic Artists, Dublin, 1984).

Parliamentary Gazetteer of Ireland (1844/5)

This is similar to Lewis's Topographical Dictionary in content and arrangement. Published in three volumes-Vol. I A-C (1845); Vol. II (D-M) (1845); Vol. III (N-Z) + index (1846). NLI Ir. 9141 p30

Ordnance Survey Field Name Books

The Ordnance Survey (OS) is Ireland's official State map-maker. The Field Name Books are the notebooks used by the surveyors compiling the first OS maps of Mayo in 1838. They are arranged by civil parish, and list each townland alphabetically. Although varying slightly between areas, the following details are usually included:

Townland name in Irish & English; Derivation of the name; Location within the parish; Proprietor's name; and other comments (See Fig X).

The original transcripts are on microfilm in the NLI, where the typescripts in hard copy are also held. The reference numbers are as follows:

Transcripts (microfilm) Pos. 4121-3
Typescripts (hard copy) Ir. 92942 03
Book no 97 -Achill-Ballintober
Book no 98 -Ballyhean-Crossboyne
Book no 99 -Crossmolina-Kilcolman
Book no 100 -Kilcommon-Kilgeever
Book no 101 -Killala-Lackan
Book no 102 -Manulla-Turlough

MAP No.	CIVIL PARISH	Alternative Name or spelling	YEAR(S) OF TITHE APP.
19	ACHILL		1828
16	ADDERGOOLE		1815, 1833
48	AGHAMORE	Aghavower	1833
70	AGHAGOWER	Aughagower	1831
24	AGLISH	Aka. Castlebar	1824
73	ANNAGH		1833
14	ARDAGH		1825
36	ATTYMASS		1834
59	BALLA	Ballagh, Bal,	1835
52	BALLINCHALLA	Ballincholla	1835
50	BALLINROBE		1827
30	BALLINTOBER		1833
27	BALLYHEAN	Ballyhane	1830
18	BALLYNAHAGLISH		1824*
34	BALLYOVEY		1830
12	BALLYSAKEERY		1829
72	BEKAN	Becan	1833
43	BOHOLA	Bucholla	1833
26	BREAGHWY	Breaffy, Breaghwee	-
31	BURRISCARRA		1833
20	BURRISHOOLE		1832
69	CASTLEMORE		1826
55	CONG		1834
63	CROSSBOYNE		1842
13	CROSSMOLINA		1833
3	DOONFEENY	Dunfeeny	1834
29	DRUM	Drummonahan	1834
46	INNISHBOFFIN	Ennisboffin	1830
23	ISLANDEADY	Islandine, Islandedin	1833
66	KILBEAGH		1825
17	KILBELFAD		1834
4	KILBRIDE	Kilbreedy	1833
61	KILCOLMAN		1824
67	KILCOLMAN		1832
2	KILCOMMON		1834
51	KILCOMMON		1833
41	KILCONDUFF		1833
5	KILCUMMIN	Kilcommin	1833
42	KILDACAMMOGE	Kildecamogue	-
7	KILFIAN	Kilfyan	1815,1833
35	KILGARVAN	Kilgarvey	1834
47	KILGEEVER	Gilgavower	1830*
10	KILLALA		1833
38	KILLASSER		1834
44	KILLEDAN	Killedin	1834
22	KILMACLASSER		1831
56	KILMAINEBEG		1836

MAP No.	CIVIL PARISH	Alternative Name or spelling	YEAR(S) OF TITHE APP.
54	KILMAINEMORE		1836
21	KILMEENA	Kilmina	1827*
53	KILMOLARA		1834
1	KILMORE		1834
15	KILMOREMOY		1834
68	KILMOVEE		1827
65	KILTURRA	Kiltora,Kilturragh	1834
64	KILVINE		-
71	KNOCK	Knockdrumcalry	1833
6	LACKAN		1833
28	MANULLA	Minola	1830,1837
60	MAYO		1827*
40	MEELICK		1833
57	MOORGAGAGH	Moorgaga	1836
11	MOYGOWNAGH	Magaunagh	1815,1834
45	OUGHAVAL	Aughaval	-
8	RATHREAGH	Rathrea	1829,1834
49	ROBEEN		-
32	ROSSLEE		1833
58	SHRULE	Shruel	1825
62	TAGHEEN	Taugheen, Taghkeen	1827*
39	TEMPLEMORE	Sraide,Strade	1833
9	TEMPLEMURRY		1834
37	TOOMORE	Towmore, Tuymore	1833
33	TOUAGHTY	Towaghty	1834
25	TURLOUGH		1825

* Only main landholders listed

Civil parishes as numbered on map.

1. Kilmore
2. Kilcommon (Erris)
3. Doonfeeny
4. Kilbride
5. Kilcummin
6. Lackan
7. Kilfian
8. Rathreagh
9. Templemurry
10. Killala
11. Moygawnagh
12. Ballysakeery
13. Crossmolina
14. Ardagh
15. Kilmoremoy
16. Addergoole
17. Kilbelfad
18. Ballynahaglish
19. Achill
20. Burrishoole
21. Kilmeena
22. Kilmaclasser
23. Islandeady (2 pts.)
24. Aglish
25. Turlough
26. Breaghwy
27. Ballyhean
28. Manualla
29. Drum
30. Ballintober (2 pts.)
31. Burriscarra
32. Rosslee
33. Touaghty
34. Ballyovey
35. Kilgarvan
36. Attymass
37. Toomore
38. Killasser
39. Templemore
40. Meelick
41. Kilconduff
42. Kildacommoge (3 pts.)
43. Bohola
44. Killedan
45. Oughaval
46. Inishboffin
47. Kilgeever
48. Aghagower
49.Robeen
50. Ballinrobe
51. Kilcommon (Kilmaine)
52. Ballinchalla
53. Kilmolara
54. Kilmainemore (2 pts.)
55. Cong
56. Kilmainebeg (2 pts.)
57. Moorgagagh
58. Shrule
59. Balla
60. Mayo
61. Kilcolman
62. Tagheen
63. Crossboyne
64. Kilvine
65. Kilturra
66. Kilbeagh
67. Kilcolman
68. Kilmovee
69. Castlemore
70. Aghamore
71. Knock
72. Bekan
73. Annagh

A list of the Civil parishes in alphabetical order and specifying the map numbers, is on pages 21 & 22.

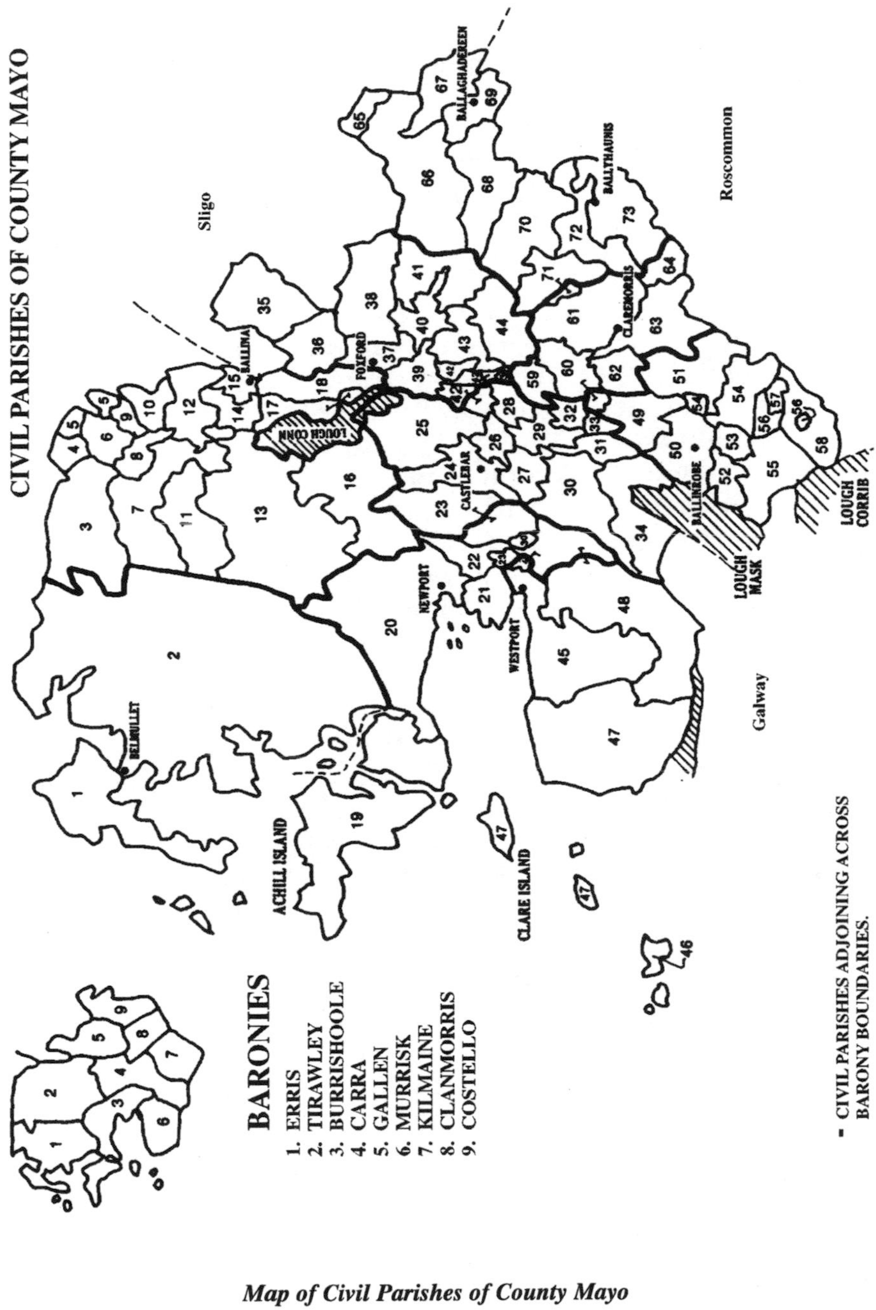

Map of Civil Parishes of County Mayo

Christchurch, Dublin; the vicarage forms part of the union of Crossmolina. The tithes amount to £250, of which £13. 10. is payable to the precentor, £111. 10. to the vicars choral, and £125 to the vicar. The R. C. parish is co-extensive with that of the Established Church; the chapel is at Laherdane. There are two public schools, in which are about 130 boys and 30 girls; and six hedge schools, in which are about 160 boys and 70 girls. There are some remains of an old abbey at Addergoole, and also at Bofinan; and near Castle Hill are vestiges of an ancient castle.

AGHAVOWER, or AGHAMORE, a parish, in the barony of COSTELLO, county of MAYO, and province of CONNAUGHT, 4½ miles (N.) from Ballyhaunis, on the road from that place to Swinford; containing 7062 inhabitants. St. Patrick is said to have erected a monastery here, for his disciple St. Loarn. The surface of the parish is varied with several small lakes; the lands are chiefly under tillage; there is a considerable quantity of bog, also a quarry of black marble. The gentlemen's seats are Cooge, the residence of James Dillon, Esq.; Annach, of Thomas Tyrrell, Esq.; and Oahil, of James McDonnell, Esq. Fairs are held at Ballinacostello on June 3rd, Aug. 8th, Oct. 19th, and Dec. 18th. The parish is in the diocese of Tuam, and is a rectory and vicarage, forming part of the union of Kiltullagh: the tithes amount to £158. 4. 10. The ancient church is in ruins, but the cemetery is still used. In the R. C. divisions it is part of the district of Knock; the chapel is an old thatched building. There are seven pay schools, in which are about 550 children. At Cloonfallagh there is a mineral spring.

ANNAGH, a parish, in the barony of COSTELLO, county of MAYO, and province of CONNAUGHT, on the road from Castlebar to Frenchpark; containing, with the post-town of Ballyhaunis, 6885 inhabitants. This place was chiefly distinguished for a cell of Franciscan friars, though by some writers said to have been founded by Walter de Burgh for brethren of the order of St.

A description of the Civil Parish of Aghamore from the Topographical Dictionary of Ireland by Samuel Lewis (1837)

Chapter 4 Civil Registration Records

One of the largest and most valuable sources available to the family history researcher are the civil registers of birth, marriage and death held by the General Register Office in Dublin.

Civil registration began in Ireland in 1845 with the recording of non Catholic marriages. It was not until 1864 that registration of all marriages, and of births and deaths commenced. The registers held by the General Register Office are as follows:

Births: All births in Ireland from Jan 1st 1864, specifying: Child's name; date & place of birth, name of father, occupation of father, name and maiden name of mother and name of the informant.

Marriages: Non-Catholic marriages from 1st Jan 1845, and all marriages from 1st Jan 1864 specifying: Place & date of marriage, name, age, address & occupation of the bride & groom, name and occupation of father of bride and groom, & witnesses to the marriage.

Deaths: All deaths in Ireland from 1st Jan 1864 specifying: Date & place of death, name of deceased, marital status, age, occupation, cause of death and details of informant.

Other useful records of possible Mayo relevance also held at the GRO are:

- Births of Irish subjects which took place at sea from 1864. From 1886 a separate index can be found in the back of the main index volume for the relevant year of registration.
- Deaths of Irish subjects which took place at sea from 1864. Separate index (as above) from 1866
- Births, Marriages and Deaths of Irish subjects serving in the British army abroad from 1880. Separate index (as above) from 1888.
- Births of Irish subjects abroad from 1864. No index is available but the registers may be inspected at the GRO Such births had to be notified to the relevant British Consul abroad.

The indexes to the above registers can be accessed in the Search Room of the GRO at 8/11 Lombard St., Dublin. The registers are not available for personal inspection, but copies of all entries can be obtained from GRO staff. A daily research fee can be paid, or a fee to view 5 years of indexes of births, marriages or deaths may be preferred.

These yearly indexes are arranged in alphabetical order by surname followed by

INDEX to BIRTHS REGISTERED in IRELAND in 1865.

Vol.	Page	Name and Registration District.	Vol.	Page	Name
6	43	LYNOTT, Thomas. Killala	9	347	LYONS, John. N
9	983	LYNSKEY, Anne. Claremorris	19	187	—— John. Ball
12	618	—— Bridget. Ballina	19	18	—— John. Listo
12	670	—— Ellen. Claremorris	14	198	—— John. Colo
17	549	—— John. Swineford	9	482	—— John. Swin
17	541	—— Margret. Claremorris	9	169	—— John. Calli
2	831	—— Martin. Gort	14	336	—— John. Cah
12	696	—— Mary. Ballinrobe	14	44	—— John. Cork
12	581	—— Mary. Swineford	14	506	—— John. Ban
15	131	—— Mary. Ballina	9	16	—— John. Don
7	806	—— Nicholas. Galway	19	290	—— John. Lon
7	648	—— Nicholas. Ballinrobe	4	53	—— John. Gler
13	121	—— Nicholas. Ballinrobe	4	58	—— John. Clar
18	94	—— Patrick. Swineford	14	509	—— John. Cast
3	226	—— Patrick John. Galway	4	302	—— John. Lisn
19	157	—— Peter. Gort	9	333	—— John. Scar
12	326	—— Thady. Tuam	19	559	—— John. Loug
12	585	—— Thomas. Mountbellew	9	416	—— John. New
1	303	LYNSKY, Honoria. Swineford	4	550	—— John. Mitc
1	319	—— James. Belmullet	9	81	—— John. Swin
13	14	—— Mary. Swineford	19	506	—— John. Tua
9	419	—— Mary. Castlebar	4	130	—— John Joseph
4	544	—— Mary. Galway	9	290	—— Joseph. Lu
11	508	—— Michael. Swineford	9	493	—— Joseph. Du
11	469	LYNUP, Anne. Castlecomer	3	541	—— Kate. Clon
11	881	LYON, Anne Jane. Rathdown	12	906	—— Lawrence.
18	108	—— Susan. Naas	2	1023	—— Margaret.
9	856	LYONS, Alexander. Donegal	7	47	—— Margaret.
14	819	—— Alice. Cavan	13	92	—— Margaret.
10	363	—— Anastasia. Clonmel	4	725	—— Margaret.
20	67	—— Andrew. Dublin, South	12	664	—— Margaret.
5	540	—— Anne. Killala	9	353	—— Margaret.
5	728	—— Anne. Glenties	2	142	—— Margaret.
10	50	—— Anne. Dundalk	17	764	—— Margret. C
20	298	—— Anne. Claremorris	14	180	—— Margret. C
5	357	—— Anne. Ennis	19	251	—— Maria. Mo
10	381	—— Anne. Claremorris	4	187	—— Maria. Dul
10	64	—— Anne Caroline. Athy	8	483	—— Martin. Ga
10	379	—— Anty. Cashel	13	489	—— Martin. Cl
20	621	—— Austin. Claremorris	14	185	—— Martin. Cl
15	299	—— Bernard. Claremorris	14	183	—— Mary. Car
5	360	—— Bridget. Athlone	8	1	—— Mary. Lon
5	392	—— Bridget. Dublin, South	7	695	—— Mary. Cro
5	373	—— Bridget. Ballinrobe	9	62	—— Mary. Kill
10	412	—— Bridget. Loughrea	9	401	—— Mary. Ban
10	728	—— Bridget. Callan	9	580	—— Mary. Nev
9	417	—— Bridget. Nenagh	18	581	—— Mary. Kan
5	544	—— Bridget. Dublin, South	2	768	—— Mary. Gle
5	545	—— Bridget. Strokestown	3	407	—— Mary. Dub
20	620	—— Bridget. Nenagh	3	639	—— Mary. Dul
5	542	—— Bridget. Ballinasloe	14	32	—— Mary. Bell
6	305	—— Bridget. Waterford	14	861	—— Mary. Kil

Column of Index to Births Registered in Ireland in 1865

forename, registration district, volume number and page number. When an entry of interest is identified, a photocopy of the entry from the relevant register, or a full certified copy, can be obtained. In the case of the death indexes, the age of the person at the time of death is also given in the index. A zero indicates that the death was of a child under 1 year of age.

Late registrations can be found in the back pages of the relevant yearly index, or in one of the following periods. Up to 1877 the indexes are in one single yearly volume. From 1878 each yearly volume has separate indexes for each of the four quarters i.e. January to March, April to June, July to September and October to December.

It is worth remembering that the indexes are based on the dates of registration of births, deaths and marriages, and not on the date of occurrence of the relevant event. It may take some time for the event to be registered. A birth, death or marriage taking place in March may therefore appear in the index for the April to June quarter. Likewise an event taking place in December may appear in the first quarter of the following year.

As explained in Chapter 3, registration occurred in Registration Districts. The Registration Districts for Co. Mayo are Ballina, Ballinrobe, Belmullet, Castlebar, Claremorris, Killala, Newport, Swineford and Westport. The Civil Registration District of Killala was amalgamated with Ballina in April 1917. Similarly Newport was amalgamated with Westport in January 1886.

Access to GRO Records

Some or all of the GRO records may be consulted at the following archives:

General Register Office, 'Joyce House' 8-11 Lombard Street, Dublin 2.
Holdings: All registers and indexes as outlined above.

Office of Superintendent Registrar, New Antrim Street, Castlebar, Co. Mayo.
Holdings: They hold only the registers of births, deaths and marriages for the districts in Co. Mayo since 1864. General searches may be made only by prior arrangement with this office.

Church of Jesus Christ of Latter Day Saints, Family History Centres (see P. 86)
Holdings: International Genealogical Index (IGI) which includes some civil registration details up to about 1867. They are arranged by county and indexed by surname. Their holdings also include civil registration indexes and copies of some civil registers.

National Library, Kildare St., Dublin 2.

1. Index to the births registered in Ireland for the years 1864, 1865 and 1866. (Call No. LB Thom 3121)

2. Deceased Seamen. 1887-1949
Names of seamen whose deaths were reported to GRO specifying: name of deceased; age; rank or profession; official number; name and type of ship; port of registry; cause; place and date of death. From 1893 it includes sex; nationality or place of birth; and last place of abode. (NLI Call no. 31242 d.).

Mayo Coroners Inquests.

The earliest surviving records of the Mayo Coroners office are 1888. However they include witness statements and verdict. The full list of surviving records are detailed in the index to the records of the Circuit court held at the NAI.

Chapter 5 Censuses, Census Substitutes & Other Sources

Census Returns:

This chapter lists and describes the official censuses conducted in Co. Mayo, and also other sources which describe a significant number of Mayo residents at a particular period.

Official Government Censuses of Ireland have been carried out at 10 year intervals since 1821. However, the individual household returns for the years 1821-1851 were destroyed in a fire in the Public Record Office in 1921. Returns for the years 1861-1871 were destroyed by Government order to protect confidentiality, and the 1881 and 1891 returns were pulped during the First World War due to a shortage of paper. A full set of returns for the 1901 & 1911 censuses are available for public inspection in the National Archives (See P. 83).

The following is a chronological list of sources for Mayo, with a description, and where each can be accessed:

1625-35. Stafford Inquisition of Co. Mayo:

Landholders and others named in an inquisition which opened in Ballinrobe on 31 July 1635. Arranged by barony with indexes of persons, places and subjects. Royal Irish Academy Ms. 24.E.15; SOG Library; Also published by the Irish Manuscripts Commission (Dublin, 1958).

1630-39. Particulars of Quarters of Land in Mayo.

Arranged by barony, it lists 54 landholders and extent of holdings. NLI Pos. 1416.

1641. Books of Survey and Distribution

Lists the owners of the land in 1640, and the owners following its confiscation and redistribution in 1641. RIA Ms 1 VI. 1; Published by Irish Manuscripts Commission (Dublin 1956).

1654 - 58. The Transplantation to Connaught:

This is arranged by county, subdivided by Barony. It lists planters, their original county and address, and holding. Also local transplantation giving name and original parish address. Pub. by the Irish Manuscripts Commission (Dublin 1970). County Mayo is covered on pp 183 - 225.

1691. Mayo Jacobites:

A list of Mayomen who were indicted and outlawed for treason against William III. Gives names, and in some cases addresses and relationships. Analecta Hibernica Vol. 22, p. 1-240.

1692-98. Foxford Quit Rent Collection Books.

Names of proprietors, locations of land, area and yearly charge. NAI M 6968.

1716. Petitioners for the Fortification of Ballinrobe:

Lists the names of 70 Protestant freeholders petitioning (in July 1716) for Ballinrobe to be fortified with surrounding walls. J. Galway Arch. & Historical Society, Vol. VII (1911-12) p. 168-70.

1783. Ballinrobe, Register of Householders

This register is arranged by street or townland and lists the names of approximately 190 householders. The names are not in alphabetical order. Analecta Hibernica, Vol. 14.

1785. Lord Altamont's Rent Roll of Westport

A list of 87 persons in the town of Westport who paid rent to Lord Altamont. It is arranged by street giving names and rent paid. In the journal 'Cathair na Mart' 1982 Vol. 2 No.1.(see Westport Hist. Soc. P. 84). .

1786. Westport Petitioners

A memorial dated March 10th 1786 calling for a regular post between Westport and Castlebar and signed by 70 local inhabitants. NAI Post Office records, MFA 43/1 Also published in Cathair na Mart No.16, 1996. (see Westport Hist Soc. P. 84).

1793 - 1794. Catholic Qualification Rolls:

Names, addresses and rank/occupation of Catholics taking an oath of allegiance in order to have restrictions against them eased. The rolls for Mayo were signed in Castlebar in July 1793 and January 1794, also in Newport in July 1793. NAI Ref. 2 - 446 - 53.

1795. Armagh Migrants to the Westport Area

A petition by Armagh migrants to Westport to the Lord Lieutenant of Ireland, seeking relief and assistance. It contains a list of 99 names only. Pub. in the journal 'Cathair na Mart' 1982 Vol. 2 (1) (see Westport Hist Soc. P. 84).

1796. Linen Board Premiums For Persons Growing Flax:

A list of persons paid premiums for sowing flax in a scheme run by the Linen Board to increase the supply of flax. It provides the name and parish of residence of over 2,000 persons in Mayo. It is available in several archives in book or microfiche versions, some of which are indexed. NLI (Call number: Ir.633411 i7); NAI; SOG Library.

1796. Catholics Migrating from Ulster to Mayo

A list of 283 persons from Antrim, Armagh, Cavan, Derry, Down, Fermanagh, Monaghan and Tyrone who immigrated into Mayo. Arranged by county (and townland if given).of origin and detailing name, location in Mayo and number in household. Seanchas Ardmhacha Vol. 3(1) 1958 p.17-50.

1798. Persons Claiming For Losses Suffered In The 1798 Rebellion

A list of `loyal' subjects claiming damages for losses sustained during the 1798 rebellion (see Chapter 13). Arranged in alphabetical order by name and providing occupation/rank, residence, and place where loss was sustained, nature of loss and amount claimed. Over 650 claims were submitted from Mayo. These claims are available in book form in the National Library (NLI. JLB.94107).

1800-1805 Families in the Townland of Carrowmore, Knock

Lists of the residents of the townland of Carrowmore & Knock from Lord Dillon's rental papers 1800-1805, the Tithe Applotments 1833, Griffith's Valuation 1856 and the 1901 census. J. of SMFRHC Vol. VII 1994 p. 22-25.

1809. Killala Organ Subscribers.

A list of subscribers to a fund to purchase a new organ for Killala Church of Ireland Cathedral. NAI MFCI 32.

1815-42 Tithe Applotment Surveys

These are extensive listings of landholders eligible for payment of tithes. Although the layout is not standard, typical details provided include name of occupier, landholding area and tithe payable. A surname index is available. See Land Records (Chapter 8) for details.

1815. Lord Sligo's Rent Roll, Westport

A list of over 200 persons in the town of Westport paying rent to Lord Sligo. Arranged by street giving names and rent paid. Pub. in 'Cathair na Mart' 1982 Vol.2 (1). (see Westport Hist Soc. P. 84).

1817. Mayo Summer Assizes

Lists the names of 17 persons sentenced to hang, giving the crime committed and date of sentence. National Archives: OP 488/24.

1818. Tithepayers of Kilfian & Moygownagh:

A list of 450 persons who paid tithes in the parishes of Kilfian and Moygownagh giving their townland of residence and amount paid. NAI (M.6085).

1818. Rent Roll of the Marquis of Sligo.

Lists 91 tenants of the Marquis of Sligo in the parishes of Aughagower, Burrishoole, Kilmeena and Oughaval. Pub. in 'Cathair na Mart' Vol. 5 (1) 1985 p. 22-24). (see Westport Hist Soc. P. 84).

1823-24. Westport Tithepayers

List of those paying tithes at the Westport Petty Sessions, 1823-24. Details include name, residence, and amount of tithe payable. NLI Ms. 14, 902

1823/24. Defendants at Westport Petty Sessions

Details of those appearing at the Westport Petty Sessions specifying; name of defendant and complainant, case of complainant, punishment awarded and whether committed, held to bail or dismissed. Addresses are given in returns of some sessions. NLI Ms. 14,902.

c. 1825. Ballina Landholders and Traders

A memorial of landholders and traders of Ballina seeking a grant to have the River Moy deepened. Over 100 signatures. National Archives: OP 974/131.

1827. Killala Tithe-payers.

Names (only) of persons paying tithes in Killala in April 1827. NAI MFCI 32.

1830/31. Voters of Co. Mayo

A list of persons entitled to vote as holders of a lease for life of a house or land with an annual rent worth £10 or more. Alphabetically arranged listing names, addresses and how they voted. Telegraph (Connaught Ranger) of 15/22 June 1831; Reprinted in SMFHRC Jnl. Vol. VII 1994. p. 6-21

1831. Petitioners of Kilgarvan and Attymass:

A list of approx. 750 names of petitioners for poor relief as a result of `the scarcity of potatoes, depression of the Linen trade and injust valuation of tithes'. A request was made to create work by finishing a road through Coolcarney (common name for Kilgarvan and Attymass). NAI: OP 974/116

1832. Protestants of Foxford & Surrounding Areas

A census of the Protestant populations of Attymass, Ballynahaglish, Foxford (Toomore), Killasser, Killedan & Templemore. Arranged by parish listing Head of households, children and other relationships. Of the 210 persons listed, 70% are from Foxford. NLI: Ms.8295

1832-39. Mayo Freeholders

A list of freeholders in Co. Mayo arranged alphabetically by name, giving address. situation & valuation of freehold, and place and date of registration, NAI: OP 1839/138

1833. Tithepayers of Kilmore Parish

Dated November 1833, this Tithe Applotment Composition Book is arranged by townland listing occupier, area of holding, valuation and some observations. NLI Ms 5933.

1833. Defendants at Mayo Lent Assizes

A list arranged by surname giving forename and crime. Published in "Claremorris in History" (Mayo Family Hist. Soc., Mayo, 1987) p. 66-77.

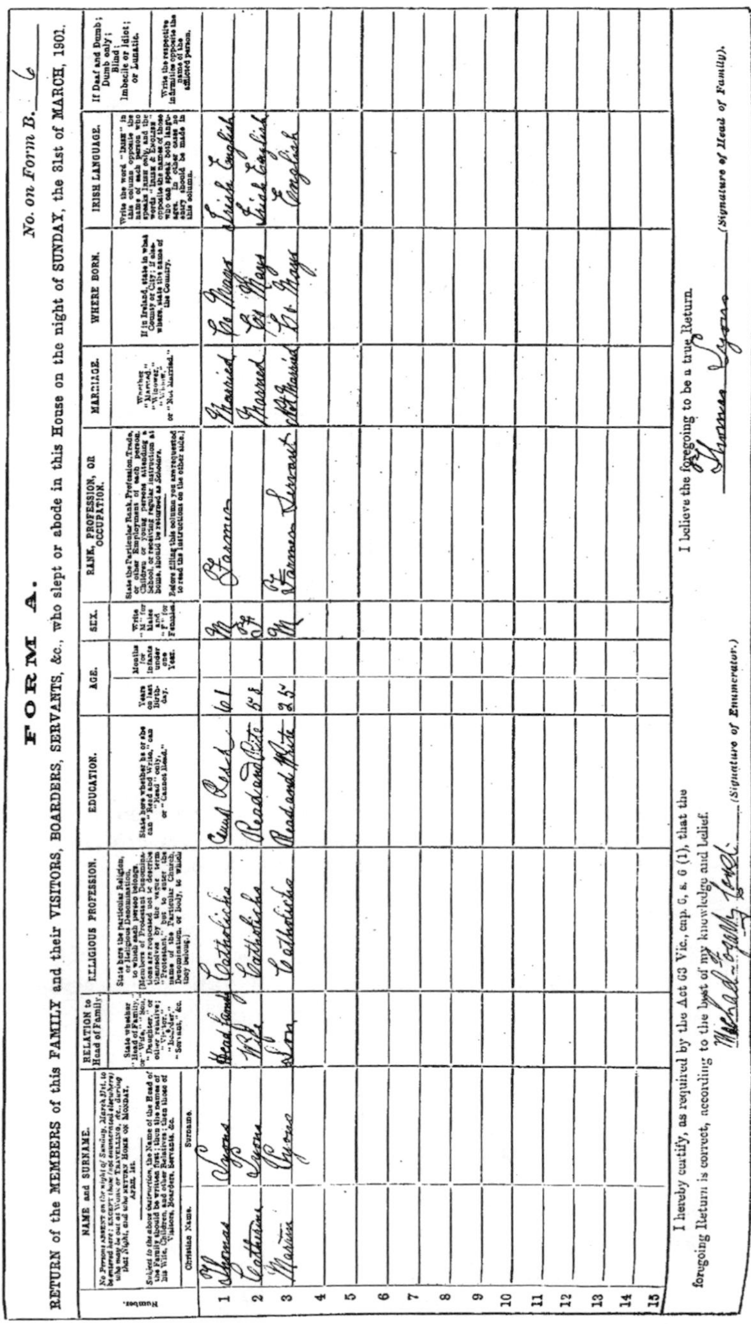

CENSUS OF IRELAND, 1901.

(Two Examples of the mode of filling up this Table are given on the other side.)

FORM A. No. on Form B. 6

RETURN of the MEMBERS of this FAMILY and their VISITORS, BOARDERS, SERVANTS, &c., who slept or abode in this House on the night of SUNDAY, the 31st of MARCH, 1901.

Number	Christian Name	Surname	Relation to Head of Family	Religious Profession	Education	Age: Years on last Birthday	Age: Months for Infants under one Year	Sex	Rank, Profession, or Occupation	Marriage	Where Born	Irish Language	If Deaf and Dumb; Dumb only; Blind; Imbecile or Idiot; or Lunatic
1	Thomas	Lyons	Head family	Catholicks	Can't Read	61		M	Farmer	Married	Co Mayo	Irish English	
2	Catherine	Lyons	Wife	Catholicks	Read and Pite	58		F		Married	Co Mayo	Irish English	
3	Martin	Lyons	Son	Catholicks	Read and Write	25		M	Farmer Servant	Not Married	Co Mayo	English	

I hereby certify, as required by the Act 63 Vic., cap. 6, s. 6 (1), that the foregoing Return is correct, according to the best of my knowledge and belief.

Michael Fogarty [illegible] (Signature of Enumerator.)

I believe the foregoing to be a true Return.

Thos. Lyons (Signature of Head of Family).

A copy of a 1901 Census Return from the townland of Corhawnagh, Aghamore.

1833. Tenants of Lord Clanmorris

Lists the names, rents payable and some observations on over 300 tenants of Lord Clanmorris. NLI Ms 3279.

1834. Tithepayers of Kilconduff Parish

Dated May 1834 this Tithe Applotment Composition Book is arranged by townland listing occupier, area, quality of land, arable value and other observations. NLI Ms 5933.

1835. Tithepayers of Kilcummin Parish

Dated November 1835, this Tithe Applotment Composition Book is arranged by townland and lists occupier, description of land, and valuations. NLI Ms 5933

1835. Mayo Chelsea Pensioners

A list of names of out-pensioners of Chelsea Hospital (British Army Veterans) residing in the county of Mayo who have been found fit at recent examinations. Details given as follows: Pensioners name, Regiment, Rate of pension and Address (Parish or Village). National Archives: OP 1835/8.

1836. Defendants at Mayo Summer Assizes

A list, arranged by surname, giving forename and crime. Published in "Claremorris in History" (Mayo Family Hist. Soc., Mayo, 1987) p. 78 -81.

1839. Crossmolina Parishioners

A list of names of 170 parishioners who nominated Messrs. Bryan Gildea and James Gallagher as applotters for the parish. NAI: Call No. OP/1839/77.

1839 Gaming Certificates List

Gaming certificates were issued to persons allowing them to hunt for game in certain areas for certain periods. A printed list of persons who obtained gaming certificates arranged by area is available in PRONI Ref.: T. 688

1842. Mayo Freeholders

A list of freeholders registered in 1842 for the baronies of Burrishoole, Carra, Clanmorris, Costello, Gallen, Kilmaine and Murrisk. Alphabetically arranged by name, giving address. situation of freehold, valuation of freehold, place and date of registration. NAI: OP 1842/71

1845. Defendants at Mayo Summer Assizes

Notebook of Hon. Justice Jackson giving the names and details of 43 cases heard before him. NAI: M.5249

1845. Tenants of Clare Island:

Names only of tenants of the Clare Island villages of Capnagower, Fawnglass, Glann, Kill, Lecarrow, Maum, Strake and Toormore. From the Telegraph (Connaught Ranger) of 3 September 1845, reprinted in SMFHRC Jnl. Vol. VII 1994 P. 46- 47

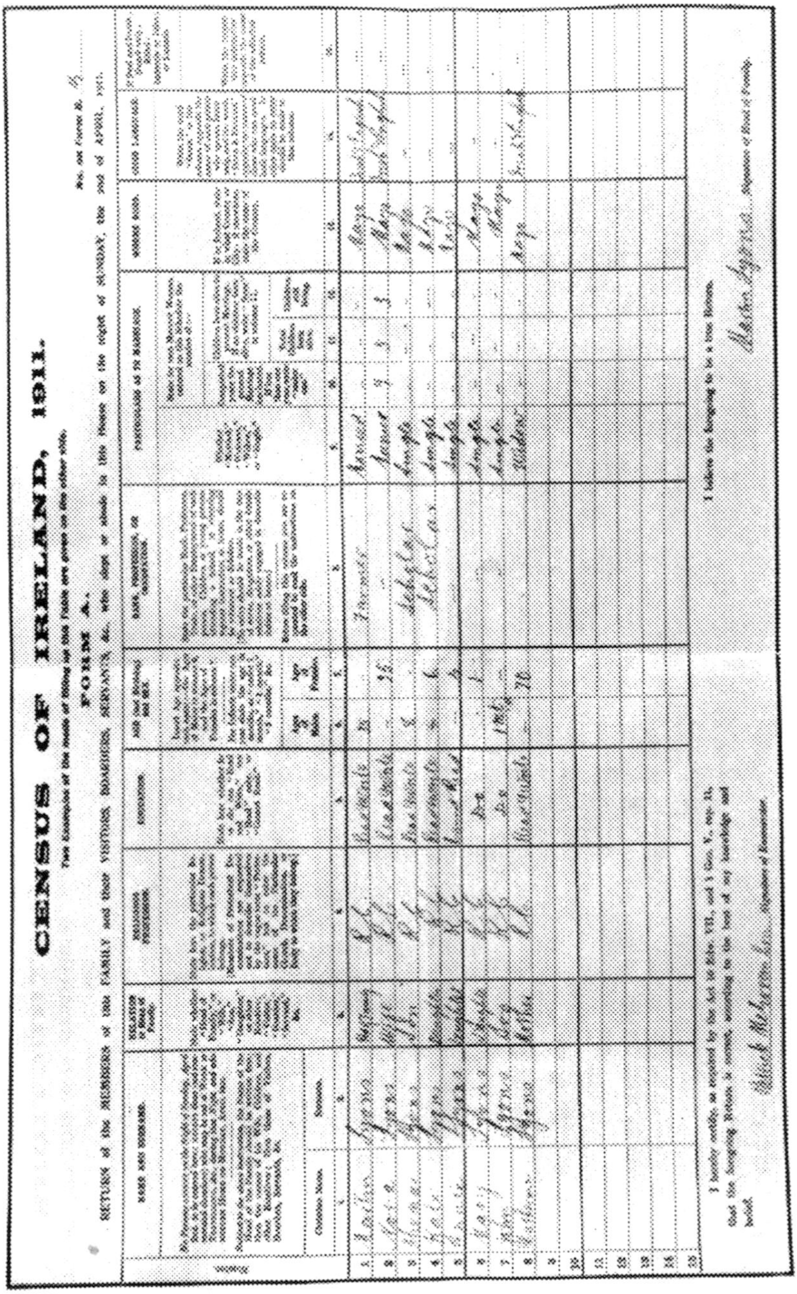
CENSUS OF IRELAND, 1911.

FORM A.

A copy of a 1911 Census Return from the townland of Corhawnagh, Aghamore.

1849. Ballina Presbyterian Church Subscription List

A small notebook containing the names of persons who subscribed to the building of the Presbyterian Church in Ballina in 1849. Only names and amount subscribed included. PHSI Library

1850. Voters of County Mayo

An alphabetical list by barony of the names of all occupiers of land, hereditaments rated separately or together at the net annual of £12 or upwards. Pub. in Jnl SMFHRC 1996, p. 27 - 41.

1851. Tenants of Clare Island etc.

Rentals of the lands and premises of the estates of Clare Island, Castleaffy, Ballynew, Kilboyne, Kilnacurra, Rosehill, Carrowmore and Caher over which a receiver was appointed in 1851. The name, townlands, yearly rents, arrears and observations of the 746 tenants are listed. NAI: M. 2795.

1852 - 54. Tenants of Ballinrobe

Index to the tenants of Mr. John Hearne, Agent for the estate of F.J. DeMontmorency. Alphabetically arranged listing 240 tenants name, townland, rent and year. SMFHRC Jnl. 1989 p. 22-26.

1855/57 Griffith's Primary Valuation

Comprehensive list of land occupiers of Mayo. Provides, for each landholding, the name of occupier, townland, the Ordnance survey map references, Description of the holding etc. A surname index is available. See Land records Chapter 8.

1855 - 72. Pupils of Lehinch National School

An index of pupils of the school including child's name, address, year of birth, parents occupation, and some comments. This school is situated on the Hollymount to Ballindine road in the townland of Lissatava. SMFHRC Jnl. 1989 p. 39-49

1856 - 1857. Mayo Voters Register

Registers of persons entitled to vote at any election of Members of Parliament for the period 1856/57. Arranged by barony giving Name, Abode, Qualification to vote, Description and location of property. The registers can be consulted at the NAI using the following call numbers: Barony of Clanmorris: M.3448. Barony of Costello: M.3447. Barony of Gallen: M.2784. Barony of Kilmaine: M.2783. Barony of Tyrawley: M.2782.

1860. Tenants of the Browne Estate.

An index to the tenants on the rental of the estate of James Browne and James Denis Howe Browne (In Crossboyne, Kilcolman and Tagheen) alphabetically arranged by name, and giving street or townland address. Pub in "Claremorris in History' p 44-51.

1878. Tenants of the Moores of Moore Hall

An index to the Rent Rolls of the Moore Hall Estate, listing names and townland. Published in Jnl. SMFHRC 1990 p. 5-15.

1881. Kiltimagh Eviction Families

10 eviction forms relating to the Brennan, Clarke, Conlon, Higgins, Kelly, Prendergast and Walsh families of Kiltimagh. Details include, tenants name, address, number in family, rent, arrears, tenancy, landlords name, agents name and observations. NLI Ms 17, 714(5)

1884. Tenants of Clare Island

A memorial of the occupiers of the Lands of Glen, Capnagower and Fawnglass on Clare Island requesting the enlargement of the harbour. It is dated 8 Sept. 1884 and contains 37 signatures. NAI: OPW 32698/84.

1894. Mayo Shareholders

Liquidator's list of shareholders in the Irish Land Purchase and Settlement Co. Ltd. Alphabetically arranged by name, giving address, occupation and number of shares or extent of interest. Dates 18 January 1894, it includes details of 90 Mayo persons. NLI MS 13, 471.

1894. Victims of the Clew Bay Disaster

A list of those who perished in the Clew Bay Disaster which occurred on the 14 June 1894. Names, age, address and marital status from a memorial at Kildavent on Achill Island. SMFHRC. Jnl. Vol. VII 1994, p. 40.

1898. Lodgers in Westport

One of the provision of the Common Lodging House Act of 1851 was that a register of lodgers be kept by the keeper of each lodging house. The register of keepers Mary Carney and Bridget Salmon both of Peter Street, Westport survives. The permits included are dated June 1898. The register contains several alphabetical lists of names only. NLI Ms 12, 700.

1901 Census Returns:

This was the official Government Census of all households conducted on Sunday the 31st of March 1901. The details given in these returns are as follows: Forename, Surname, Relationship to Head of family, Religion, Literacy, Age, Sex, Occupation, Marital Status, Birthplace, Ability to speak Irish, and Infirmities. These returns are available in the NAI and copies are held in Mayo County Library in Castlebar. (see p. 33).

1901. Mayo Persons Residing in Kingstown, Dublin

An alphabetically arranged list of Mayo persons who were residing in Kingstown (Dun Laoghaire) during the compilation of the 1901 census. Details include, name, address, age, religion, marital status and occupation. Published in the Journal of the Dun Laoghaire Genealogical Soc., Vol. 5. (2) 1996, p. 71-74; Vol. 5 (3) 1996, p. 116.

1901. Achill Parish; Census Index

An index to the 1901 census returns for the parish of Achill including transcripts of the originals. Published by William G. Masterson (Indianapolis, 1994) NLI Ir. 94123 m21

1903. Tenants of the Burke Property

This rental gives the following details: Name of tenant; Yearly rent; Area; Description of tenancy and observations for the townlands of Corrahoor, Attavally and Carrick, all in the barony of Gallen. It relates to a High Court order regarding the selling of land. NAI: M.3699

1908 - 1922. Census Search Applications

The Pension act of 1908 allowed for persons of 70 years and over to receive an 'old-age' pension. As the civil registration of births only began in 1864, birth certificates were not available as proof of age. A common method of proving age was to apply for a search of the household return for the applicants home in one of the early censuses (usually those of 1841, 1851 or 1861). This should show the applicant and give his age at the time of the particular census searched, and would (where relevant) prove the applicants eligibility for pension payment.

The applicants details were completed on census search application forms, also known as Green Forms. These search forms are held in the NAI, and are indexed by the county, barony, parish and townland in which the search was made. Each gives the name of the family who were claimed to be resident in the census. The Green form provides the following details: Name and address of applicant; Name of parents of applicant (with maiden name of mother if given); Name of head of family if other than father; Relationship and occupation; Year of census to be searched; Parish; Townland/Street and date of receipt of application. Held in NAI; Copies are also held at the PRONI (Belfast): T.550

1911 Census Returns:

This was the official Government Census of all households conducted on 2nd of April 1911. Each household return gives the following details for each occupant: Forename, Surname, Relationship to Head of family, Religion, Literacy, Age, Occupation, Marital Status, Number of years married, Birthplace, Languages spoken (i.e. Irish and/or English) and Infirmities. Of particular relevance is that it states, (for each married woman) the number of children born, and the number then alive. Held in NAI. (see p. 35).

1913-1923. Irish Army Medal Applications:

Medals were awarded for services during the Irish War of Independence, but only after application was made and merit established. Application details include: Name, 1916-1923 service units, districts and references. Requests for searches can be made in writing to: Veterans Allowances Section, Department of Defence, Renmore, Co. Galway.

1914 - 1918. Irishmen who died in the First World War.

These memorials are of Irishmen in Irish and British regiments of the British Army who lost their lives in the Great European War of 1914 - 1918. Details were compiled and published in 1923 by the Irish National War Memorials Commission. The 49,400 entries provide: Name; Regiment number; Rank; Battalion; Place of death; Date of death and, in the majority of entries, the place of birth. A copy of these records was placed in every major Irish library.

1918. Mayo Voters List

A list of Persons entitled to vote at Parliamentary and Local elections. Voters name are listed alphabetically within voting districts, giving address and qualification to vote. NAI 1D-51-77/80.

1922. Irish Army Census

A census of personnel of the Army of the new Irish State carried out in November 1922. These returns provide: name, address, next of kin, date of attestation and age. The above returns are held at the Military Archives, Cathal Brugha Barracks, Rathmines, Dublin 6. (By prior appointment only).

Additional Records of Wider Time Periods.

In addition to the above sources, there are also some further records which are either undated, or for a wide time period:

Mill Books:

These are undated lists (by Barony) of millers and details of their premises, and include 57 Mayo millers. They are available in the National Archives. There is no reference number for these books , they may be inspected by simply requesting "Mill Books". This source has been published in "The Millers and Mills of Ireland… of about 1850' by William E. Hogg (Dublin 1997).

1703 - 1838. Convert Rolls:

A index by surname of over 5,500 people who converted from Catholicism to the Church of Ireland during the period 1703 - 1838. These Convert Rolls were edited and indexed by Eileen O'Byrne and published by the Irish Manuscripts Commission (Dublin 1981) Mayo converts were published in MNFHRC (1997) pp 33-38. (see p. 76).

1814 - 1922. Royal Irish Constabulary:

The Irish police force came into being as the Irish Peace Preservation Force in 1814. In 1836 the Irish Constabulary was formed, and was renamed the Royal Irish Constabulary in 1867. During its existence some 90,000 men enrolled. The records of all of these are held by the Public Record Office in London and a microfilm copy is available in the NAI. The records are indexed by the initial letter of the surname of the member in two periods i.e. 1816-67 and 1867-1922. They contain the following details: Name; Age when appointed; Height; Native County; Religion; Date of marriage; Native county of wife; and Dates of appointments, allocations, transfers, promotions; rewards/marks of distinction etc., punishments etc. It also specifies when discharged, Dismissed, Resigned, Dead or Pensioned. The index and details can be consulted at the NAI (Ref. MFA 24/1-16) or Public Record Office. London (Ref. HO 184.43) . RIC. Directories for the years 1840-45, 1857, 1876-79 and 1881-1921 are also available at the National Library.

1888 - 1988. Shraigh School Rolls:

This lists all the children on the school rolls in the period 1888-1988. It includes the date of admission, name of child and townland. Published in the `Shraigh Centenary Year Book' (Ballina; Western People 1988)

1906 - 1979. Students of St. Muirdeacha's College, Ballina.

A roll of students arranged by: (1) Year with name and address (2) Surname index with forename and year of enrolment. National Library: Ir.259 m2.

1924 - . Irish Army Pension Applications:

Applications for Irish Army Pensions, providing name and details of service . A search of these records can be made by post only, giving as much details known as possible, to: Veterans Allowances Section, Department of Defence, Renmore, Co. Galway.

Chapter 6 Church Records

As civil registration of births, marriages and deaths only began in 1864, (and non-Catholic Marriages in 1845) we are dependent on the various churches (denominations) for records of these events prior to these dates.

All denominations have their own parish structures and practices for recording of baptisms, marriages and (sometimes) deaths/burials. The quality and availability of records varies between these different denominations. The factors that determine when record-keeping started, and what records were kept, are fully explored in 'Irish Church Records' (Flyleaf Press, Dublin 1992).

In Mayo the major denominations are Roman Catholic (almost 97% of the population in 1861); and Church of Ireland (2.6% of the population). Other denominations represented only 0.6% of the population in that year, and few records of Presbyterian, Methodist, Baptist and other churches therefore exist. A search of neighbouring parish registers should be considered when an ancestor is proving difficult to locate.

Listed below are the surviving church records arranged by civil parish, indicating the time-frame for record availability, and the repositories in which they are held.

Roman Catholic

Roman Catholic records are recorded by parish, which are grouped into dioceses, of which there are three in Mayo, i.e. Achonry, Killala and Tuam. One parish, Shrule, is within the diocese of Galway.

Mayo Catholic records are relatively sparse in comparison to many Irish counties, for a variety of reasons. The earliest surviving Baptismal register starts in 1802, and earliest Marriage register in 1791. Only three parishes recorded deaths, i.e. Kilfian, Killasser and Kilmoremoy. Most of the post-1870 marriage registers record the names of the mothers of the marrying couple, a detail omitted from civil marriage certificates.

In addition to the individual parish records, a composite index of registers of marriages (for 1821 and 1822, with additions in some parishes to 1829) in each deanery of the diocese of Tuam has been published by Murphy and Reilly (Maryland, 1993). The original is at NLI Pos 4222.

Note that some Catholic parishes have alternate names, either because there were several chapels of different names, or because they had one official name, and another common name. The original records are all in their parish of origin, and may be inspected there with the permission of the parish priest. However, most have also been indexed by one of the 2 Heritage Centres that operate in the county (see P xxx); and these will conduct a search of their indexes for a fee. The records which have been indexed by these centres are indicated below. In addition, almost all of the records are available on microfilm in the NLI, and in the Mormon Family History Libraries. (SLC).

Civil Parish: Achill
Catholic Parish: Achill
Bapt: 12.1867-12.1880 NLI (mf); 1868-1900 MNFHRC (index)
Marr: 10.1867-6.1880 NLI (mf); 1867-1900 MNFHRC (index)

Civil Parish: Addergoole
Catholic Parish: Addergoole
Bapt: 1.1840-12.1880 NLI (mf); 1840-1899 MNFHRC (index)
Marr: 1.1840-3.1878 NLI (mf); 1840-1900 MNFHRC (index)

Civil Parish: Aghagower
Catholic Parish: Aghagower
Bapt: 4.1828-5.1836; 3.1842-12.1880 NLI (mf); 1828-1900 SMFHRC (index)
Marr: 11.1854-12.1880 NLI (mf); 1828-1900 SMFHRC (index).

Civil Parish: Aghamore
Catholic Parish: Aghamore
Bapt: 2.1864-9.1880 (Modern transcript) NLI (mf); 1864 - 1900 SMFHRC (index)
Marr: 12.1864-9.1880 NLI (mf); 1864-1900 SMFHRC (index)

TUAM DIOCESE LDS BFA 1279206 #13-15
1864-1901
1864-1921

Civil Parish: Aglish
Parish Register: Castlebar, Ballyhean, Breaghwy
Bapt: 1.1838-12.1880 (in disorder to 4.1855)NLI (mf);1839-1900 SMFHRC (index)
Marr: 6.1824-4.1843; 6.1843-12. 1880 NLI (mf); 1824-1900 SMFHRC (index)

Civil Parish: Annagh
Catholic Parish: Annagh/Ballyhaunis
Bapt: 11.1851-12.1880 NLI (mf);1851-1900 SMFHRC (index)
Marr: 6.1852-6.1870; 11.1870-12.1880 NLI (mf); 1851-1900 SMFHRC (index)

Civil Parish: Ardagh
Catholic Parish: Ardagh
Bapt: 2.1870-7.1880 NLI (mf);1866-1900 MNFHRC (index)
Marr: 1882-1900 MNFHRC (index)

Civil Parish: Attymass
Catholic Parish: Attymass
Bapt: 6.1875-8.1880 NLI (mf); 1875-1900 MNFHRC (index)
Marr: 2.1874-10.1880 NLI (mf); 1874-1897 MNFHRC (index)

Civil Parish: Balla
Catholic Parish: Balla, Manulla, Drum, Roslee
Bapt: 5.1837-12.1880 NLI (mf); 1837-1900 SMFHRC (index)
Marr: 7.1837-10.1880 NLI (mf); 1837-1900 SMFHRC (index)

Civil Parish: Ballinchalla *see Cong*

Civil Parish: Ballinrobe
Catholic Parish: Ballinrobe
Bapt: 8.1843-4.1856; 1.1861-12.1880 NLI (mf); 1853-1900 SMFHRC (index)
Marr: 10.1850-4.1856, 1.1861-11.1880 NLI (mf); 1847-1900 SMFHRC (index)

Civil Parish: Ballintober
Catholic Parish: Burriscarra & Ballintober
Bapt: 9.1839-12.1880 NLI (mf); 1839-1900 SMFHRC (index)
Marr: 9.1839-3.1880 NLI (mf); 1839-1900 SMFHRC (index)

Civil Parish: Ballyhean *see Aglish*

Civil Parish: Ballynahaglish
Catholic Parish: Backs:
Rathduff:
Bapt: 8. 1848-12.1859 & 1.1861-9.1879 NLI (mf);
Marr: 12.1848-4.1860 & 1.1865-12.1869 & 2.1874-9.1879 NLI (mf);
Knockmore:
Bapt: 10.1854-10.1856, 3.1858-8.1879 NLI (mf); 1825-1900 MNFHRC (index)
Marr: 9.1860-11.1861, 1.1869-7.1879 NLI (mf); 1815-1894 MNFHRC (index)

Civil Parish: Ballyovey
Catholic Parish: Partry
Bapt: 10.1869-7.1878 NLI (mf); 1869-1900 SMFHRC (index)
Marr: 1.1870-7.1878 NLI (mf); 1847-1900 SMFHRC (index)

Catholic Parish: Tourmakeady
Bapt: 8. 1869-12.1880 NLI (mf);
Marr: 1869-9. 1880 NLI (mf) (Modern transcript)

Civil Parish: Ballysakeery
Catholic Parish: Ballysakeery
Bapt: 11.1843-12. 1880 NLI (mf); 1844-1881 MNFHRC (index)
Marr: 10.1843-12.1880 NLI (mf); 1843-1881 MNFHRC (index)

Civil Parish: Bekan
Catholic Parish: Bekan
Bapt: 8.1832-2.1844 & 12.1844-5.1871 NLI (mf); 1832-1900 SMFHRC (index)
Marr: 5.1832-5.1872 NLI (mf)(pages missing);1832-1900 SMFHRC (index)

Civil Parish: Bohola
Catholic Parish: Bohola
Bapt: 10.1857-12.1880 NLI (mf); 1857-1900 MNFHRC (index)
Marr: 10.1857-5.1880 NLI (mf); 1857-1900 MNFHRC (index)

Civil Parish: Breaghwy *see Aglish*
Civil Parish: Burriscarra *see Ballintober*

Civil Parish: Burrishoole
Catholic Parish: Burrishoole/Newport
Bapt: 1872-1900 MNFHRC (index)
Marr: 1.1872-11.1880 NLI (mf); 1872-1900 MNFHRC (index)

Civil Parish: Castlemore *see Kilcoleman (Costello)*

Civil Parish: Cong
Catholic Parish: Cong & The Neale
Bapt: 2.1870-12.1880 (Modern transcript)NLI (mf); 1870-1900 SMFHRC (index)
Marr: 1870-1900 SMFHRC (index)

Civil Parish: Crossboyne
Catholic Parish: Crossboyne & Tagheen
Bapt: 7.1862-2.1877 (Modern transcript) 5.1877-12.1880 NLI (mf); 1835-1900 SMFHRC (index)
Marr: 1.1877-7.1880 NLI (mf); 1791- 1900 SMFHRC (index)

Civil Parish: Crossmolina
Catholic Parish: Crossmolina
Bapt: 8.1831-8.1841, 4.1845-12.1880 NLI (mf); 1831-1900 MNFHRC (index)
Marr: 11.1832-2.1841, 3.1846-12.1880 NLI (mf); 1832-1900 MNFHRC (index)

Civil Parish: Doonfeeny
Catholic Parish: Ballycastle
Bapt: 8.1864-12.1880 NLI (mf); 1853-1900 MNFHRC (index)
Marr: 1.1869-9.1880 NLI (mf); 1869-1900 MNFHRC (index)

Civil Parish: Drum *see Balla*

Civil Parish: Innisboffin
Catholic Parish: Innishboffin
Bapt: 10.1867-12.1880 NLI (mf);
Marr: 11.1867-10.1880 NLI (mf);

Civil Parish: Islandeady
Catholic Parish: Islandeady
Bapt: 9.1839-5.1876 NLI (mf); 1839-1900 SMFHRC (index)
Marr: 9.1839-9.1880 NLI (mf); 1839-1900 SMFHRC (index)

Civil Parish: Kilbeagh
Catholic Parish: Kilbeagh
Bapt: 1.1855-12.1880 NLI (mf); 1847-1900 MNFHRC (index)
Marr: 5.1845-3.1866, 1.1855-9.1880 (different records) NLI (mf); 1844-1900 MNFHRC (index)
Catholic Parish: Carracastle
Bapt: 1.1853-12.1880 NLI (mf); 1863-1900 MNFHRC (index)
Marr: 7.1847-11.1880 NLI (mf);1847-1900 MNFHRC (index)

Civil Parish: Kilbelfad *see Ballynahaglish*
Civil Parish: Kilbride *see Doonfeeny*

Civil Parish: Kilcolman (Bo. Clanmorris)
Catholic Parish: Kilcolman/Claremorris
Bapt: 4.1835-1.1838, 3.1839-5.1873 NLI (mf); 1835-1900 SMFHRC (index)
Marr: 6.1806-2.1830, 1.1835-3. 1836, 12.1838-6.1871 NLI (mf); 1805-1900 SMFHRC (index)

Civil Parish: Kilcolman (Bo. Costello)
Catholic Parish: Castlemore & Kilcolman
Bapt: 11.1851-12.1880 ,1861 and 1864-1872 (Modern transcript) NLI (mf); 1851 - 1911
Marr: 8.1830-10.1867, 2.1868-11.1880 NLI (mf); 1830 - 1963
LDS - BFA 1279232 # 1-9
Achonry Diocese

Civil Parish: Kilcommon (Bo. Erris)
Catholic Parish: Gweesalia
Bapt: 1883-1900 MNFHRC (index)
Marr: 1886-1900 MNFHRC (index)

Catholic Parish: Kiltane
Bapt: 8. 1860-12. 1880 NLI (mf); 1860-1900 MNFHRC (index)
Marr: 9. 1860-3. 1880 NLI (mf); 1860-1900 MNFHRC (index)

Catholic Parish: Kilcommon-Erris
Bapt: 1883-1900 MNFHRC (index)
Marr: 1843-1900 MNFHRC (index)

Catholic Parish: Belmullet
Bapt: 2.1841-12.1880 NLI (mf); 1841-1900 MNFHRC (index)
Marr: 1.1836-5.1845, 8.1857-11.1880 NLI (mf); 1836-1900 MNFHRC (index)

Catholic Parish: Ballycroy
Bapt: 1885-1900 MNFHRC (index)
Marr: 1890-1900 MNFHRC (index)

Catholic Parish: Bangor/Aughoose
Bapt: 1853-1861 MNFHRC (index)
Marr: 1854-1860 MNFHRC (index)

Civil Parish: Kilcommon (Bo. Kilmaine)
Catholic Parish: Kilcommon & Robeen
Bapt: 10.1857-12.1880 NLI (mf); 1857-1900 SMFHRC (index)
Marr: 10.1857-6.1880 NLI (mf); 1857-1900 SMFHRC (index)

Catholic Parish: Kilcommon/Roundfort
Bapt: 12.1865-12.1880 NLI (mf);
Marr: 11.1865-4.1880 NLI (mf);

Civil Parish: Kilconduff
Catholic Parish: Kilconduff and Meelick
Bapt: 3.1822-6.1826, 5.1841-12.1900 NLI (mf); 1822-1900 MNFHRC (index)
Marr: 6.1808-3.1878, 4.1878-11.1915 NLI (mf); 1808- 1878 MNFHRC (index)

Civil Parish: Kilcummin *see Lackan*

Civil Parish: Kildacommoge
Catholic Parish: Keelogues
Bapt: 8.1847-12.1880 NLI (mf); 1847-1900 MNFHRC (index)
Marr: 8.1847-9.1880 NLI (mf); 1847-1900 MNFHRC (index)

Civil Parish: Kilfian
Catholic Parish: Kilfian
Bapt: 10.1826-4.1836 NLI (mf); 1826-1836 MNFHRC (index)
Marr: 7.1826-10.1844 NLI (mf); 1826-1836 MNFHRC (index)
Death: 10.1826-2.1832 NLI (mf);

Civil Parish: Kilgarvan
Catholic Parish: Kilgarvan
Bapt: 3.1870-12.1880 NLI (mf); 1870-1900 MNFHRC (index)
Marr: 11.1844-5.1880 NLI (mf); 1897-1900 MNFHRC (index)

Civil Parish: Kilgeever
Catholic Parish: Kilgeever/Louisburgh
Bapt: 2.1850-3.1869 (Modern transcript), 8.1872-12.1880 NLI (mf); 1850-1900 SMFHRC (index)
Marr: 1850-1900 SMFHRC (index)

Catholic Parish: Clare Island
Bapt: 10.1851-11.1880 NLI (mf);

Civil Parish: Killala
Catholic Parish: Killala
Bapt: 4.1852-8.1873, 9.1873-12.1880 NLI (mf); 1852-1900 MNFHRC (index)
Marr: 12.1873-11.1880 NLI (mf); 1873-1900 MNFHRC (index)

Civil Parish: Killasser
Catholic Parish: Killasser
Bapt: 11.1847-12.1880 NLI (mf); 1848-1900 MNFHRC (index)
Marr: 12.1847-6.1880 NLI (mf); 1847-1900 MNFHRC (index)
Death: 11.1847-6.1848 NLI (mf);

Civil Parish: Killedan
Catholic Parish: Killedan/Kiltimagh
Bapt: 2.1861-12.1880 NLI (mf); 1861-1900 SMFHRC
Marr: 11.1861-8.1880 NLI (mf); 1834-1900 SMFHRC (index)

Civil Parish: Kilmaclasser *see Kilmeena*
Civil Parish: Kilmainbeg *see Kilmainemore*

Civil Parish: Kilmainemore TUAM DIOCESE
Catholic Parish: Kilmaine
Bapt: 6.1854-12.1880 NLI (mf); 1854-1900 SMFHRC (index)
Marr: 5. 1855-10.1877 NLI (mf); 1854-1900 SMFHRC (index)
LDS - BFA 1279214, #3-4, 0926225 2-4

Civil Parish: Kilmeena
Catholic Parish: Kilmeena
Bapt: none held on mf.

Civil Parish: Kilmolara *see Cong*

Civil Parish: Kilmore KILLALA DIOCESE
Catholic Parish: Kilmore-Erris
Bapt: 6.1860-12.1880 NLI (mf); 1859-1900 MNFHRC (index)
Marr: 9.1860-11.1880 NLI (mf); 1860-1900 MNFHRC (index)

LDS BFA 1279205 #17-18

Civil Parish: Kilmoremoy
Catholic Parish: Kilmoremoy
Bapt: 5.1823-10.1836, 5.1849-7.1849, 7.1851-9.1867, 2.1868-2.1879 NLI (mf); 1823-1900 MNFHRC (index)
Marr: 5.1823-10.1842, 10.1850-12.1880 NLI (mf); 1823-1900 MNFHRC (index)
Death: 4.1823-8.1836, 9.1840-5.1844 NLI (mf);

Civil Parish: Kilmovee
Catholic Parish: Kilmovee
Bapt: 2.1854-12.1880, 6.1854-12.1880 NLI (mf)(not same records): 1824-1900 SMFHRC (index)
Marr: 11.1824-8.1848,10.1854-5.1880 NLI (mf); 1854-1900 SMFHRC (index)

Civil Parish: Kilturra
Catholic Parish: Kilshalvey, Kilturra & Cloonoghill
Bapt: 1.1842-12.1877 NLI (mf)(some gaps pre-1852)
Marr: 4.1833-4.1876 NLI (mf)

Civil Parish: Kilvine *see Crossboyne*

Civil Parish: Knock
Catholic Parish: Knock
Bapt: 12.1868-12.1880 NLI (mf); 1868-1900 SMFHRC (index)
Marr: 9.1875-12.1880 NLI (mf); 1874-1900 SMFHRC (index)

Civil Parish: Lackan
Catholic Parish: Lackan
Bapt: 8.1852-11.1874 NLI (mf); 1852-1900 MNFHRC (index)
Marr: 3.1854-2.1869 NLI (mf) (Modern transcript, some pages missing); 1854-1900 MNFHRC (index)

Civil Parish: Manulla *see Balla*

Civil Parish: Mayo
Catholic Parish: Mayo Abbey
Bapt: 4.1841-12.1880 NLI (mf); 1841-1900 SMFHRC (index)
Marr: 9.1841-6.1880 NLI (mf); 1841-1900 SMFHRC (index)

Civil Parish: Meelick *see Kilconduff*
Civil Parish: Moorgagagh *see Kilmainemore*

Civil Parish: Moygownagh
Catholic Parish: Moygownagh
Bapt: 1887-1900 MNFHRC (index)
Marr: 1881-1900 MNFHRC (index)

Civil Parish: Oughaval
Catholic Parish: Aughaval/Westport
Bapt: 7.1845-11.1858, 1.1859-12.1880 NLI (mf); 1823-1900 SMFHRC (index)
Marr: 4.1823-2.1861, 1.1862-12.1880 NLI (mf); 1823-1900 SMFHRC (index)
Catholic Parish: Drummin and Lecanvey
Bapt: 4.1872-12.1880 NLI (mf);

Civil Parish: Rathreagh *see Kilfian*
Civil Parish: Robeen *see Kilcommon (Kilmaine)*
Civil Parish: Rosslee *see Balla*

Civil Parish: Shrule
Catholic Parish: Shrule
Bapt: 7.1831-8.1864 NLI (mf); 1832-1900 SMFHRC (index)
Marr: 7.1831-6.1848 , 10. 1855-5. 1864 NLI (mf); 1832-1900 SMFHRC (index)

Civil Parish: Tagheen *see Crossboyne*

Civil Parish: Templemore ACHONRY DIOCESE
Catholic Parish: Templemore
Bapt: 1888-1900 MNFHRC (index)
Marr: 5.1872-3.1880 NLI (mf); 1872-1900 MNFHRC (index)
LDS BFA 0926021
Civil Parish: Templemurry *see Killala*

Civil Parish: Toomore ACHONRY DIOCESE
Catholic Parish: Foxford
Bapt: 12.1871-1.1880 NLI (mf); 1871-1900 MNFHRC (index) 1871-1893
Marr: 4.1833-3.1840 NLI (mf); (MF); (Modern transcript, for original see Kilturra);1.1870-12.1880 NLI (mf); 1870-1900 MNFHRC (index) 1833-1911
LDS-BFA-12792031 #18-19
Civil Parish: Touaghty see Ballintober

Civil Parish: Turlough
Catholic Parish: Turlough
Bapt: 8.1847-12.1880 NLI (mf); 1847-1899 MNFHRC (index)
Marr: 8.1847-6.1880 NLI (mf); 1849-1900 MNFHRC (index)

Church of Ireland

The Church of Ireland dioceses are Achonry, Killala and Tuam. The earliest records start in the mid 1700's. Burials were recorded for most parishes, and these augment Civil records of death which only began in 1864. A full account of the types of records kept by the CoI is given by Raymond Refausse in 'Irish Church Records' (Flyleaf Press, Dublin, 1992).

A significant number of CoI records were destroyed in a fire in the Public Record Office in 1922. However copies and abstracts of the lost registers exist for many parishes. Original (or sole copies) of Church of Ireland registers may be in one of several places. They may be in Local Custody (LC) in the parish of origin. They are usually accessible by arrangement with the local clergyman. They may also be in the Representative Church Body Library (RCBL-see P. 84), where they are accessible for research. Finally they may be in the NAI, which also has an extensive collection of abstracts of registers. There are extensive gaps in these NAI records and only the start and end date are noted below. The records, and their access, are as follows:

Civil Parish: Achill
CoI Parish: Achill
Bapt: 1854-1896 RCBL
Marr: 1855-1936 RCBL
Burl: 1854-1877 NAI MFCI 33/34
CoI Parish: Dugort
Bapt: 1838-1866 NAI MFCI 33
Marr: 1838-1889 NAI MFCI 33; 1845-1888 RCBL
Burl: 1838-1874 NAI MFCI 33

Civil Parish: Addergoole ***see Crossmolina***

Civil Parish: Aghagower
CoI Parish: Aghagower
Bapt: 1801-1892 NAI MFCI 33; 1825-1892 RCBL
Marr: 1802-1846 NAI MFCI 33; 1828-1904 RCBL
Burl: 1826-1893 NAI MFCI 33; 1828-1893 RCBL

CoI Parish: Knappagh
Bapt: 1855-1875 NAI MFCI 32
Marr: 1855-1952 RCBL
Burl: 1855-1871 NAI MFCI 32

CoI Parish: Aghagower/Knappagh
Bapt: 1810-1900 SMFHRC (Index)
Marr: 1810-1900 SMFHRC (Index)
Burl: 1825-1900 SMFHRC (Index)

CoI Parish: Aasleagh
Bapt: 1875-1900 SMFHRC (Index)
Marr: 1859-1900 SMFHRC (Index): 1859-1956 RCBL
Burl: 1879-1926 SMFHRC (Index)

Civil Parish: Aghamore
CoI Parish: Kiltullagh (Co. Roscommon)
Bapt: 1822-1875 LC
Marr: 1822-1875 LC
Burl: 1822-1875 LC

Civil Parish: Aglish
CoI Parish: Castlebar
Bapt: 1840-1900 SMFHRC (Index)
Marr: 1845-1900 SMFHRC (Index)
Burl: 1848-1900 SMFHRC (Index)

Civil Parish: Annagh ***see Aghamore***
Civil Parish: Ardagh ***see Kilmoremoy***
Civil Parish: Attymass ***see Kilmoremoy***
Civil Parish: Aughaval ***see Oughaval***

Civil Parish: Balla
CoI Parish: Balla
Bapt: 1871-1900 SMFHRC (Index)
Marr: 1878-1900 SMFHRC (Index)
Burl: 1887-1900 SMFHRC (Index)

Civil Parish: Ballinchalla
CoI Parish: Ballinchalla
Bapt: 1831-1835 RCBL; 1831-1839 SMFHRC (Index)
Marr: 1832-1917 RCBL; 1832-1919 SMFHRC (Index)
Burl: 1831-1836 RCBL; 1831-1836 SMFHRC (Index)

Civil Parish: Ballinrobe
CoI Parish: Ballinrobe
Bapt: 1796-1872 NAI MFCI 34; 1796-1912 RCBL; 1796-1900 SMFHRC (Index)
Marr: 1809-1846 NAI MFCI 34; 1809-1862 RCBL; 1796-1900 SMFHRC (Index)
Burl: 1809-1875 NAI MFCI 34; 1809-1974 RCBL; 1796-1900 SMFHRC (Index)

Civil Parish: Ballintober ***see Balla &Drum***

BAPTISMS solemnized in the Parish of Oughavale in the County of Mayo in the year 1865

When Baptised.	When Born.	Child's Christian Name.	Parent's Name. Christian.	Parent's Name. Surname.	Abode.	Quality, Trade, or Profession.	By whom the Ceremony was performed.
1865 Feb 22 1865 No. 61	Feb 20 1865	Eliza	Robert & Eliza	McNabb	Ardigoman	Farmer	Allan James Nesbitt Curate
1865 March 29th No. 62	March 16 1865	Sarah	George & Ann	Shaw	Westport	Labourer	Allan James Nesbitt Curate
1865 April 23 No. 63	March 31 1865	Louisa Mary	John Edmund & Isabella	Whaite	Westport	Adjutant of South Mayo Militia	Allan James Nesbitt Curate
1865 May 11 No. 64	1865 March 25	Ellen Elizabeth	John & Lydia Jane	[illegible]	Westport	Corn-merchant	[illegible]
1865 May 19 No. 65	1865 Mar 16	Susan	John & Ann	Gibbons	Westport	Labourer	Allan James Nesbitt Curate
1865 July 2 No. 66	March 19 1865	Thomas William	Thomas & Mary Ann	Deniston	Westport	Land agent	[illegible]
1865 Sep 17 No. 67	Sep 10 1865	Sarah Jane	William & Jane	Ormsby	Carrowbawn	Farmer	William McCausland Clk
1865 Oct 4 No. 68	Sep 13 1865	Charles Frederick Zacharias	William & Amelia	Gray	Westport	Coast Guard	Allan James Nesbitt Curate

A page from the 1865 CoI Baptismal Register of Oughaval, Co. Mayo

Civil Parish: Ballyhean
CoI Parish: Ballyhean
Marr: 1875-1900 SMFHRC (Index)
Burl: 1855-1880 SMFHRC (Index)

Civil Parish: Ballynahaglish ***see Kilmoremoy***

Civil Parish: Ballyovey
CoI Parish: Ballyovey
Bapt: 1879-1951 RCBL; 1879-1900 SMFHRC (Index)
Marr: 1854-1954 RCBL; 1854-1900 SMFHRC (Index)
Burl: 1880-1966 RCBL; 1880-1900 SMFHRC (Index)

Civil Parish: Ballysakeery
CoI Parish: Ballysakeery
Bapt: 1802-1871 NAI MFCI 32; 1802-1899 MNFHRC (Index)
Marr: 1802-1863 NAI MFCI 32; 1802-1900 MNFHRC (Index)
Burl: 1802-1875 NAI MFCI 32

Civil Parish: Bekan ***see Aghamore***
Civil Parish: Bohola ***see Templemore***
Civil Parish: Breaghwy ***see Aglish***
Civil Parish: Burriscarra ***see Ballyhean and Ballyovey***

Civil Parish: Burrishoole: Lost

Civil Parish: Castlemore
CoI Parish: Castlemore
Bapt: 1890 -1911 RCBL
Marr: 1847-1908 RCBL

Civil Parish: Cong
CoI Parish: Cong
Bapt: 1746-1871 NAI MFCI 32; 1746-1863 RCBL;1746-1900 SMFHRC (Index)
Marr: 1745-1849 NAI MFCI 32; 1745-1956 RCBL;1845-1900 SMFHRC (Index)
Burl: 1736-1872 NAI MFCI 32; 1745-1863 RCBL; 1746-1900 SMFHRC (Index)

Civil Parish: Crossboyne
CoI Parish: Crossboyne
Bapt: 1877-1924 RCBL; 1747-1900 SMFHRC (Index)
Marr: 1854-1937 RCBL; 1854-1900 SMFHRC (Index)
Burl: 1879-1973 RCBL; 1873-1900 SMFHRC (Index)

Civil Parish: Crossmolina
CoI Parish: Crossmolina
Bapt: 1768-1872 NAI MFCI 32; 1768-1899 MNFHRC (Index); 1768-77, 1802-3 SOG, 1768-1817 SLC film 897365
Marr: 1768-1844 NAI MFCI 32; 1769-1899 MNFHRC (Index); 1769, 1775-77, 1802-21 SOG, 1758-1823 SLC film 897365
Burl: 1768-1872 NAI MFCI 32; 1876-1899 MNFHRC (Index); 1768-77, 1802-21, SOG, 1758-1823 SLC film 897365

Civil Parish: Doonfeeny
CoI Parish: Ballycastle
Bapt: 1842-1899 MNFHRC (Index)
Marr: 1844-1899 MNFHRC (Index)
Burl: 1877-1899 MNFHRC (Index)

Civil Parish: Drum
CoI Parish: Belcarra
Bapt: 1877-1900 SMFHRC (Index)
Marr: 1845-1928 SMFHRC (Index)
Burl: 1879-1900 SMFHRC (Index)

Civil Parish: Innishboffin
CoI Parish: Ballinakill, Co. Galway
Bapt: 1775-1914 RCBL
Marr: 1792-1928 RCBL
Burl: 1803-1951 RCBL

Civil Parish: Islandeady ***see Aglish***
Civil Parish: Kilbeagh: Lost
Civil Parish: Kilbelfad ***see Kilmoremoy***
Civil Parish: Kilbride: ***see Doonfeeny***

Civil Parish: Kilcolman (Bo. Clanmorris)
CoI Parish: Kilcolman/Claremorris
Bapt: 1877-1932 RCBL; 1877-1932 SMFHRC (Index)
Marr: 1846-1949 RCBL; 1846-1949 SMFHRC (Index)
Burl: 1878-1969 RCBL; 1878-1969 SMFHRC (Index)

Civil Parish: Kilcolman (Bo. Costello) ***see Castlemore***

Civil Parish: Kilcommon (Bo. Erris)
CoI Parish: Ballycroy
Marr: 1855-1898 RCBL
Burl: 1883-1962 RCBL

CoI Parish: Belmullet
Bapt: 1877-1900 MNFHRC (Index)
Burl: 1877-1900 MNFHRC (Index)

Civil Parish: Kilcommon (Bo. Kilmaine)
CoI Parish: Kilcommon
Bapt: 1921-1926 RCBL
Marr: 1845-1937 RCBL;1845-1937 SMFHRC (Index)
Burl: 1920-1959 RCBL

Civil Parish: Kilconduff: Lost
Civil Parish: Kilcummin: Lost
Civil Parish: Kildacommoge ***see Aglish & Turlough***
Civil Parish: Kilfian ***see Crossmolina***
Civil Parish: Kilgarvan ***see Kilmoremoy***

Civil Parish: Kilgeever
CoI Parish: Louisburgh
Bapt: 1877-1900 SMFHRC (Index)
Marr: 1846-1952 RCBL; 1846-1900 SMFHRC (Index)
Burl: 1810-1970 SMFHRC (Index)
Also; Bulnahinch Marr: 1854-1873 RCBL

Civil Parish: Killala
CoI Parish: Killala
Bapt: 1757-1871 NAI MFCI 31/32; 1810-1900 MNFHRC (Index);1757-1769 SOG; SLC film 897365; 1757-1769
Marr: 1758-1842 NAI MFCI 31/32; 1704-1900 MNFHRC (Index);1759-1767 SOG; SLC film 897365; 1757-1767
Burl: 1758-1871 NAI MFCI 31/32; 1838-1900 MNFHRC (Index); 1757-1798 SOG; SLC film 897365; 1757-1772

Civil Parish: Killasser: *see Toomore*
Civil Parish: Killedan: *see Toomore*
Civil Parish: Kilmaclasser *see Oughaval*
Civil Parish: Kilmainebeg *see Kilmainemore*

Civil Parish: Kilmainemore
CoI Parish: Kilmaine
Bapt: 1744-1927 RCBL & NAI MFCI 31/32; 1744-1900 SMFHRC (Index)
Marr: 1744-1891 RCBL & NAI MFCI 31/32; 1744-1900 SMFHRC (Index)
Burl: 1744-1908 NAI MFCI 31/32; 1744-1958 RCBL; 1744-1948 SMFHRC (Index)

Civil Parish: Kilmeena
CoI Parish: Kilmeena
Bapt: 1887-1904 RCBL
Marr: 1845-1917 RCBL

Civil Parish: Kilmolara *see Ballinchalla & Cong*

Civil Parish: Kilmore
CoI Parish: Kilmore/Binghamstown
Bapt: 1877-1900 MNFHRC (Index)
Civil Parish: Kilmoremoy
CoI Parish: Ardnaree/Ballina
Bapt: 1769-1874 NAI MFCI 34; 1770-1900 MNFHRC (Index);1768-1820 SOG; 1768-1817 SLC film 897365
Marr: 1769-1846 NAI MFCI 34;1770-1900 MNFHRC (Index);1768-1823 SOG; 1768-1815 SLC film 897365
Burl: 1769-1867 NAI MFCI 34; 1871-1900 MNFHRC (Index); 1768-1823 SOG; 1768-1821 SLC film 897365

Civil Parish: Kilmovee *see Castlemore*

Civil Parish: Kilturra
CoI Parish: Emlafad (Co. Sligo)
Bapt: 1831-1875 NAI;1762-1882 RCBL
Marr: 1831-1845 NAI;1762-1875 RCBL
Burl: 1831-1875 NAI; 1762-1941 RCBL

Civil Parish: Kilvine *see Crossboyne*

Civil Parish: Knock *see Aghamore*
Civil Parish: Lackan Lost
Civil Parish: Manulla *see Balla*

Civil Parish: Mayo
CoI Parish: Mayo
Marr: 1849-1862 RCBL

Civil Parish: Meelick Lost
Civil Parish: Moorgagagh *see Kilmainemore*
Civil Parish: Moygawnagh *see Crossmolina*

Civil Parish: Oughaval or Aughaval
CoI Parish: Westport
Bapt: 1820-1872 NAI MFCI 33; 1801-1887 RCBL;1801-1900 SMFHRC (Index)
Marr: 1820-1845 NAI MFCI 33;1802-1854 RCBL;1802-1900 SMFHRC (Index)
Burl: 1820-1908 NAI MFCI 33; 1820-1903 RCBL; 1820-1900 SMFHRC (Index)

Civil Parish: Rathreagh *see Ballysakeery*
Civil Parish: Robeen *see Kilcommon (Kilmaine)*
Civil Parish: Rosslee *see Balla*

Civil Parish: Shrule
CoI Parish: Shrule
Bapt: 1854-1863 RCBL

Civil Parish: Tagheen *see Kilcommon (Kilmaine)*
Civil Parish: Templemore *see Toomore*
Civil Parish: Templemurry Lost

Civil Parish: Toomore
CoI Parish: Foxford
Bapt: 1844-1900 MNFHRC (Index)
Marr: 1844-1900 MNFHRC (Index)

Civil Parish: Touaghty *see Balla, and Drum*

Civil Parish: Turlough
CoI Parish: Turlough
Bapt: 1821-1872 NAI MFCI 36; 1810-1900 SMFHRC (Index)
Marr: 1822-1851 NAI MFCI 36; 1810-1900 SMFHRC (Index)
Burl: 1822-1873 NAI MFCI 36; 1810-1900 SMFHRC (Index)

Presbyterian Church

There was only a tiny population of Presbyterians in Mayo at any time. According to Samuel Lewis's Topographical Dictionary (1837) only 4 parishes had Presbyterian worship. This figure increased steadily showing most records starting about the mid 1860's. Presbyterian marriages can be found in the civil registers from 1845. Burial records were rarely kept and CoI burial records should be checked. A useful source of background information is 'A History of Congregations in the Presbyterian Church of Ireland, 1610-1982' PHSI (Belfast, 1982).

Aglish (Castlebar)
Marr: 1897 MNFHRC (Index) & SMFHRC (Index)

Aughaval (Westport)
Bapt: 1858-1900 MNFHRC (Index) & SMFHRC (Index);
1825-1858 PHSI
Marr: 1850-1898 MNFHRC (Index) & SMFHRC (Index);
1825-1857 PHSI

Ballina (Kilmoremoy)
Bapt: 1846-1900 MNFHRC (Index)
Marr: 1851-1899 MNFHRC (Index)

Ballycastle (Doonfeeny)
Bapt: 1849-1900 MNFHRC (Index)
Marr: 1851-1896 MNFHRC (Index)

Ballysakeery
Bapt: 1848-1900 MNFHRC (Index)
Marr: 1837-1899 MNFHRC (Index)

Clogher
Bapt: 1873-1918 PHSI

Hollymount (Kilcommon)
Bapt: 1854-1920 PHSI
Marr: 1862-1911 PHSI

Newport (Burrishoole)
Bapt: 1850-1900 MNFHRC (Index)
Marr: 1859-1890 MNFHRC (Index)

Turlough
Bapt: 1819-1900 MNFHRC (Index)
Marr: 1819-1898 MNFHRC (Index)
Burl: 1856-1899 MNFHRC (Index)

Methodist Church (Wesleyan):

Methodist church records for Mayo are administered through the Enniskillen and Sligo district where the originals of extant records are stored. These are noted 'Sligo' below. They are not available for public inspection but queries may be addressed in writing to: Superintendent Minister, Methodist Manse, Ardaghowen, Co. Sligo. As there is a close connection between Methodists and Church of Ireland, the records of the latter should be also consulted. Below is a list of available Methodist records.

Ballina
Bapt: 1836- Sligo; 1838-1900 MNFHRC (Index)
Marr: 1864- Sligo; 1864-1900 MNFHRC (Index)

Castlebar
Bapt: 1829-1954 Sligo; 1829-1901 MNFHRC (Index)
Marr: 1868-1943 Sligo

Crossmolina
Marr: 1866-1871 Sligo
Marr: 1866-1871 MNFHRC (Index)

Erris (Belmullet)
Bapt: 1851-1861 Sligo
Bapt: 1851-1861 MNFHRC (Index)

Killala
Bapt: 1854-1866 Sligo
Bapt: 1852-1866 MNFHRC (Index)

Westport
Bapt: 1853-1954 Sligo
Marr: 1864-1897 Sligo

Chapter 7 Wills, Administrations & Marriage Licences

Wills and Administrations

A Will is the written instructions of a deceased person as to the division of their assets after their death. The maker of the will (the testator) will usually specify the distribution of the property, and appoint a trusted person (the Executor) to carry out their instructions. To achieve a legal status, a will must be accepted, or 'proven' by a Probate court. If a deceased person died without making a will (i.e. intestate), this court must do so on their behalf, taking account of their assets, and the family and creditor situation. This is called an Administration. On certain occasions where a will has been made but it is inoperable (eg the executor is also deceased) an Administration may also be made. In these cases, the court appoints an Administrator, usually a relative or legal person, to oversee the distribution of the estate of the deceased as determined by the court. The Administrator enters a bond for a sum of money as a surety that the instructions of the court will be carried out. These bonds are called Administration Bonds

Wills and administrations can provide the researcher with excellent information on family relationships. The details can sometimes resemble a brief family pedigree. The Probate records available to researchers are as follows:

Original Wills & Administrations: These are potentially important legal documents with a particular relevance in proving ownership of property. They are stored in many different archives, as well as in private collections. The major collection of Irish wills was unfortunately destroyed in the Public Record Office fire in 1922.

Abstracts: For various legal and family history purposes, details of the persons and properties mentioned in certain wills have been abstracted and either published or otherwise made available for consultation.

Indexes: Although a large proportion of Irish wills have been destroyed, the index to the collection survives, and provides name, residence and date of death of each testator. Indexes for existing wills obviously also survive, and are usefully detailed.

Pre-1858 Wills & Administrations

Prior to 1858 Probate administration was the responsibility of the Church of Ireland, and all wills were proven in either the Prerogative court in Armagh, or a Diocesan or Consistorial court in each diocese.

The Prerogative Court (The Prerogative Court of the Archbishop of Armagh) was responsible for the proving of wills of persons whose property lay within two or more diocese's where the value in the second diocese was £5 or more. Such wills were generally those made by more wealthy individuals. However, landholders whose property straddled the border of two dioceses may also be included.

The Diocesan, or Consistorial, Court was responsible for the proving of wills of persons whose property lay within one diocese. Each Mayo diocese, ie Killala, Achonry and Tuam Diocese, had its own court.

Post 1858 Wills & Administrations

Following the abolition of the Ecclesiastical Courts (Prerogative and Diocesan) in 1857, a civil court system was established. It comprised a Principal Registry and eleven District Registries. The Principal Registry effectively replaced the Prerogative Court and dealt with cases where the testator held property in more than 1 District Registry. The District Registries replaced the Diocesan Courts. Mayo wills are proved in the District Registry of Ballina. The surviving records from each of these courts are listed below:

Surviving Pre 1858 Material of the Prerogative Court

Prerogative Will Books:

All original Prerogative wills were destroyed in 1922. However, some will books (Books into which original wills were transcribed) did survive as follows:

1664-1684; 1706-1708; 1726-1729 (All names); 1777 (Surnames beginning A-L only); 1813 (Surnames beginning with K-Z only); 1834 (Surnames beginning A-E only). These are in the NAI and indexed in the NAI Testamentary Card Index.

Prerogative Will Indexes

The indexes to Prerogative Wills also survive and are arranged alphabetically by surname giving testator's address, occupation and year of probate. The original manuscript index for the period 1536-1857 is available in the NAI. An index for the period 1536-1810, edited by Sir Arthur Vicars, was published as the 'Index to the Prerogative Wills of Ireland' (Dublin 1897); Reprinted by Genealogical Publishing Co., (Baltimore 1989). (See p. 53).

Abstracts and Sketch Pedigrees

Biographical details from a huge collection of pre-1800 Prerogative Wills and Administrations were abstracted by William Betham before their destruction. These abstracts are in the NAI. Betham also constructed sketch pedigrees, based on these abstracts, which are in the GO. Copies are held by the SOG.

Irish Wills in Canterbury

An Index to the Abstracts of Wills of Irish Testators registered in the Prerogative Court of Canterbury 1636-1698 is held in the Manuscript Reading Room of the NLI (Ms. 1397).

Prerogative Administration Grant Books:

All original grants (Letters of Administration) were also destroyed and only a few Grant Books (books into which original grants were transcribed) survived. They are as follows: 1684-1688; 1748-1751; 1839. Also: 1784-1788 (Prerogative Day Books)

These are held at the NAI.

1777 **Kirwan**, Annabell, Galway town, widow
1640 ,, Andrew, Fitzpatrick, Galway, alderman
1773 ,, Andrew, Galway
1786 ,, Andrew Fitzwilliam
1802 ,, Andrew, Miltown
1780 ,, Bridget, widow of Ambrose K.
1790 ,, Bridget, Galway town, widow
1811 ,, Bridget, Frenchgrove, co. Mayo, widow
1807 ,, Edmond, Dalgin, co. Galway, esq.
1787 ,, Elizabeth, Galway, widow
1800 ,, Hyacinth, major in Galway militia
1781 ,, John, formerly of Castlehacket, now of Dublin, esq.
1794 ,, John Anthony, Galway town, merchant
1791 ,, Julian, Galway, spinster
1809 ,, Margery, Castletown, widow (Copy)
1759 ,, Mark, Galway, gent.
1755 ,, Martin, Dalgin, co. Mayo, esq.
1807 ,, Martin, Frenchgrove, co. Mayo, esq.
1789 ,, Mary, Dublin, widow
1795 ,, Mary, Hillsbrook, co. Galway, widow
1802 ,, Mary, Milltown, co. Mayo, wid.
1754 ,, Patrick FitzThomas, Galway, merchant
1758 ,, Patrick, Cregg, co. Galway, esq.
1766 ,, Patrick, Tuam, co. Galway, gent.
1770 ,, Patrick, Fitzpierce, Tuam, co. Galway, merchant
1794 ,, rev. Patrick, Dublin, clerk
1795 ,, Patrick, Claremont, co. Mayo
1798 ,, rev. Patrick, Galway town
1797 ,, Peter, formerly par. priest, Izon, in France
1759 ,, Richard, Currastoonmoore, co. Roscommon, gent.
1779 ,, Richard, Woodfield, co. Galway, esq.
1776 ,, Robert, titular bishop of Achonry, co. Sligo
1794 ,, Sophia Hamilton, Dublin, wid.
1733 ,, Thomas Fitzpatrick, Galway, merchant
1797 ,, Thomas, Galway town, esq.
1810 ,, Thomas, Isle of Man (Copy)
[See KERWAN.]

1804 **Kissane**, William, Scallihene, co Tipperary
1660 **Kitching**, Richard, Dublin, gardener [VIII. 71
1640 **Kitchinman**, Thomas, London, mercer (Copy)
1767 **Kittrick**, Walter, Dublin, publican
1781 **Kittson**, George, Prussia-st., Dubl., gent.
1794 ,, Richard, surgeon's mate of 28th regt. of foot
1766 **Knabbs**, John
1787 **Knapp**, Bridget, Dublin, widow
1791 ,, Edmond, Cork, alderman
1762 **Knapton**, John, lord baron
1724 **Knaresborough**, Michael, Waterford, merchant
1796 ,, Michael, Kilkenny city, esq.
1735 ,, Oliver, Dublin, merchant
1789 ,, Robert, Dungarvan, co. Waterford, gent.
1785 ,, William, Kilkenny city, gent.
1635 **Knatchbull**, Vincent, Killahie, co. Kilkenny, esq.
1736 **Knauge**, Mathew, Flesstown, co. Roscommon, esq.
1784 **Knight**, Andrew, Corcummins, co. Monaghan, gent.
1794 ,, Ann, Broomfield, co. Cavan, spinster
1736 ,, Bulstrode Peachy, par. St. Ann, esq.
1728 ,, Christopher, Ballynoe, co. Cork, gent.
1782 ,, Christopher, Charleville, co. Cork, gent.
1799 ,, Christopher Henry, Brickfield, co. Limerick
1805 ,, sir Christopher, Limerick city, knt.
1789 ,, Edmond, Castlebar, co. Mayo, merchant [co.
1740 ,, Francis, Maryborough, Queen's
1773 ,, Henry, Maryborough, Queen's co., gent.
1691 ,, James, Dublin, gent.
1726 ,, James, Dublin, gent.
1740 ,, James, Dublin, glazier
1767 ,, Jas., D.D., rector of Drumragh, co. Tyrone
1700 ,, John, Cork, mariner
1720 ,, Joseph, Chiswick, Middlesex, esq. (Copy)
1775 ,, Mary, Dublin, widow
1742 ,, lieut. Richard, Donegal, co.

A page from Sir Arthur Vicar's Index to Prerogative Wills of Ireland 1536 – 1810. (Dublin 1897)

Prerogative Grant Indexes:

A combined index of Prerogative Grants of Administrations, Probate of Wills and Marriage Licences for the period 1595-1858. Alphabetically arranged under initial letter of surname listing name, address, occupation/condition year and nature of grant. The index is available in the NAI.

Registry of Deeds

A sizeable number of wills were registered in the Registry of Deeds. Abstracts of wills registered there during the period 1708-1832 have been published in 3 volumes 'Registry of Deeds, Dublin: Abstracts of Wills' by the IMC: Vol. 1 1708-45 (Dublin 1954); Vol. II 1746-1785 (Dublin 1956) both edited by P.B. Eustace, and Vol. III 1785-1832 (Dublin 1984) Ed. E. Ellis & P.B. Eustace.

Surviving pre 1858 material of the Diocesan Courts of Mayo:

Diocesan or Consistorial Wills Indexes: The original wills and will books for the courts covering Co. Mayo were destroyed. However, the following indexes survive:

Killala & Achonry	1756-1831: NAI (badly damaged)
Killala & Achonry	1698-1838: pub in Ir. Gen. Vol. 3 (12) (1967) p. 506-519
Tuam	1648-1858: NAI (damaged)
Tuam	1621-1821: RIA: Ms. 24. D. 16

Microfilm copies of the NAI indexes are also available in the NLI.

Diocesan Administration Bond Indexes: The original administration bonds for the Mayo Diocesan Courts did not survive but the indexes to these bonds are available as follows:

Killala and Achonry	1779-1858 NAI
Killala and Achonry	1782-1856 Ir. Anc. Vol. 7 (1) (1975) p. 55-61
Tuam	1692-1857 NAI

Microfilm copies of the NAI indexes are also available in the NLI.

Surviving Post 1858 material of the Principal Registry

Principal Registry Will Books: 1874 (Names beginning G-M); 1878 (A-Z); 1891 (G-M); 1896 (A-F); 1922 (A-Z)

Principal Registry Grant Books: 1878; 1883; 1891; 1893

The above books are held in the NAI.

Surviving Post 1858 material of Ballina Probate district:

Ballina Probate District Will Books: August 1865-December 1899; NAI, SLC film 100925-6 January 1914-August 1919; July 1923-1952 NAI

Testamentary Card Index

Having identified an entry from one of the above indexes, the Testamentary card index in the NAI should be consulted to establish if the particular will or administration survives. This index covers all surviving pre and post 1858 testamentary material (except the surviving post 1858 probate district will books). Betham's abstracts and other abstract collections are indexed separately to the main testamentary card index.

Yearly Calendars of Wills and Administrations

Yearly 'Calendars' of Wills, starting in 1858, are also held at the NAI. These are effectively abstracts of wills from 1858 on, and are printed in large bound volumes which provide the researcher with the deceased person's name, address, date of death, place of death, occupation and value of estate. The grantee's name, address and relationship is also found and the date and place of probate or administration. When an entry of interest is identified, the testamentary card index or surviving will book should then be consulted.

A Guide to Copies and Abstracts of Irish Wills

This publication compiled by the Rev. Wallace Clare (Sharman 1930) is a valuable aid to the researcher, as it provides a single alphabetical index to the following:

(a) Copies and abstracts of Irish wills deposited in the Society of Genealogists, London.
(b) Copies of wills in all the Prerogative will books which were salvaged from the PRO fire
(c) Early original wills deposited in English archives.
(d) Copies and abstracts of wills published in some historical and genealogical journals, family histories etc.

The book arrangement is as follows: name, address, date of probate and key to one of the above.

Index to Will Abstracts in the Genealogical Office.

This index is arranged alphabetically by surname giving forename, address, occupation, date and key to collection. Pub. in Analecta Hibernica Vol 17, P. 151-348.

Wills at Irish Land Commission.

An index to wills (mainly 19th c) is available. See Chapter 8.

Banns & Marriage Licences

There were several methods available to the churches to ensure that there was no impediment to a marriage. The first was the 'Banns'. This involved reading, or posting, an announcement of the intention of a couple to marry. The Banns effectively gave 3 weeks public notice of the impending marriage so any objections could be made. The Banns were read in the parish church of each of the marrying couple and in the church in which the marriage would take place if the couple were marrying elsewhere. For whatever reason, marriage by Banns was regarded as an indication of poverty by many and was avoided by most couples. Instead, a fee would be paid to the CoI minister to have the Banns waived.

The alternative, a Marriage License was obtained (prior to 1858), from the Ecclesiastical courts noted previously. It involved a payment which technically was a surety to indemnify the church against any damages that may be sought later as a result of any unforeseen impediment to the marriage. These sureties were called Marriage Licence Bonds.

Two types of marriage licences were issued:

(a) Diocesan Marriage Licences, which were valid for three months and allowed the couple to marry immediately.

(b) Prerogative Marriage Licences, which were issued by the Prerogative Court of Armagh and allowed the couple to marry anywhere with no time restrictions. Prerogative marriage licences were also known as Special Licences.

No records of Marriage Licences or Bonds survive for Mayo. Records of Banns exist in 2 CoI churches, Oughaval (1819-25) and Aughagower (1826-29), but provide no additional details to the marriage records. Indexes to the Marriage Licence Bonds do survive (in the NAI, NLI and GO) as follows:

Indexes to Marriage Licence Bonds:

Prerogative Marriage Licence Bonds Indexes
1750-1861 NAI (Alphabetically arranged by surname)
1629-1858 GO Ms. 605-607

Diocesan Marriage Licence Bonds Indexes:

The diocesan court indexes is alphabetical are arranged by surname of both bride and bridegroom, and show the full names of both parties and the year. Those available are:
Killala & Achonry Diocesan Court (1787-1842): NAI, also NLI Pos. 1882
Tuam Diocesan Court (1769-1845) NAI, also NLI Pos. 1884

Chapter 8 Land Records

In a primarily agricultural country, ownership or use of land was highly important. In addition, it was a major political issue as dispossession of land, and on occasion its planting with settlers, had widely occurred. Various land records exist. To understand these records, it is useful to know that land could be owned outright, leased on a long-term basis (for a period of years or for the duration of the lives of specified persons), or rented on a short-term basis (very often at the whim of the landlord or his agent). During the 18th and early 19th century, the occupiers of the land were generally not its owners. They were small farmers and cottiers who rented or leased the land from large estates. The major land records and their significance is described below

Record/Source	Period	What is recorded
Registry of Deeds	1708-present	Sale, mortgage, lease etc of land
Tithe Applotment Survey	1815-1842	Landholders eligible for tithe payment
Griffith Valuation Survey	1855-57	All occupiers of land
Land Commission	1881-present	Old & new owners of redistributed land
Congested Districts Board	1891 -	Some residents of Congested districts
Encumbered Estates Court	mid 1800's	Insolvent estate owners, & tenants
Estate Records	All periods	names of tenants, agents & workers
Land Registry	1897 -	Owners of land

Tithe Applotment Survey

Tithes were taxes levied on arable land for the upkeep of the CoI. Prior to 1832 they were paid 'in kind' in the form of farm produce etc. From that year a Commissioner was appointed for each parish to oversee valuation of properties and 'applotment' of tithes based on that valuation. The Tithe Applotment (or Composition) Books produced show: townland, name of occupier, area and tithe payable. A surname index is combined with the Griffith's Valuation Surname index (see below). Copies are in the NAI (NAI), the NLI and the Gilbert Library. See Parish List (p. 21) for dates.

Griffith's Primary Valuation

Griffith's Primary Valuation was carried out in Mayo between 1855 & 1857. Its purpose was to calculate a relative 'valuation' of each holding. A tax, commonly called 'rates', was levied based on this valuation. The resulting records show, for each landholding, the following: Parish and Townland; Map reference; Name of occupier; Description of the holding (or 'tenement'); Area; Rateable value of property. An index has been compiled by the NLI, and is available in many archives. It is particularly useful in locating a person within Mayo. Many Irish names are associated with one area, and a search of the index may

Valuation of Tenements.

ACTS 15 & 16 VIC., CAP. 63, & 17 VIC., CAP. 8.

COUNTY OF MAYO.

BARONY OF COSTELLO.

UNION OF SWINEFORD.

PARISH OF AGHAMORE.

No. and Letters of Reference to Map.	Names. Townlands and Occupiers.	Names. Immediate Lessors.	Description of Tenement.	Area.	Rateable Annual Valuation. Land.	Rateable Annual Valuation. Buildings.	Total Annual Valuation of Rateable Property.
				A. R. P.	£ s. d.	£ s. d.	£ s. d.
	BALLINA-COSTELLO. (Ord. S. 81.)						
1 a	James Freeman,	Margaret M. Beaty,	Land, house, & offices,	15 0 18	2 0 0	0 5 0	2 5 0
b	Thomas Freeman,	Same,	Land and house,		2 0 0	0 5 0	2 5 0
2 a	Bartholomew Fleming,	Same,	Land and house,	3 1 6	3 0 0	0 5 0	
– b			One cottage,	—	—	0 5 0	4 10 0
3 —	Bartholomew Fleming,	Same,	Land,	2 3 38	1 0 0	—	
4 a	John Kilroy,	Same,	Land, &c., & corn-kilns,	23 0 8	6 0 0	0 10 0	8 10 0
5 a	John Kilroy,	Same,	Land and corn-mill,	3 1 23	0 10 0	1 10 0	
6 a	Michael Mannion,	Same,	Land and house,	7 0 35	3 15 0	0 5 0	4 0 0
7 a	John Lyons,	Same,	Garden, house, & office,	0 2 5	0 5 0	0 10 0	3 15 0
8 —	John Lyons,	Same,	Land,	6 2 30	2 0 0	—	
9 a	Hugh Feehely,	Same,	Land, house, and office,	17 [illegible] 8	1 0 0	0 10 0	1 10 0
10 a	Patrick Lyons,	Same,	Land and house,	3 3 35	1 10 0	0 5 0	1 15 0
– b	Thomas Duffy,	Same,	House,	—	—	0 3 0	0 3 0
11 a	William Moran,	Same,	Land and house,	3 0 4	1 10 0	0 5 0	1 15 0
12 —	Michael Lyons, sen.,	Same,	Land,	1 0 8	0 5 0	—	0 5 0
13 a	Michael Lyons, sen.,	Same,	Land and house,	18 0 8	3 10 0	0 10 0	4 0 0
b	Michael Lyons,	Same,	Land and house,		3 10 0	0 10 0	4 0 0
14 a	Jeremiah Loftus,	Same,	Land and house,	8 0 38	3 0 0	0 10 0	3 10 0
15 a	Edmond Judge,	Same,	Land, house, and office,	6 0 15	3 0 0	0 5 0	3 5 0
16 a	Thomas Lyons,	Same,	Land and house,	4 0 18	1 10 0	0 5 0	1 15 0
17 —	Margaret Beaty,	In fee,	Land (fair green),	2 3 0	—	—	—
–	Margaret Beaty,	In fee,	Customs of fairs,	—	—	—	10 0 0
– a	John M'Donnell,	Margaret Beaty,	House and forge,	—	—	0 10 0	0 10 0
– b	Mary M'Donnell,	Same,	House,	—	—	0 5 0	0 5 0
			Total,	134 0 30	59 5 0	7 10 0	68 15 0
	CASHELTOURLY. (Ord. S. 81.)						
1 a	Francis R. O'Grady,	Sir Compton Domvile, Bart.,	Land, house, and offices,	270 3 37	90 0 0	0 15 0	90 15 0
2 a	Edmond M'Loughlin,	Francis R. O'Grady,	Land and house,	10 0 10	1 0 0	0 5 0	1 5 0
b	Lucky Loughan,	Same,	Land and house,		1 0 0	0 5 0	1 5 0
3 a	Thomas Higgins,	Sir Compton Domvile, Bart.,	Land and house,	13 3 38	3 15 0	0 5 0	4 0 0
4 —	Patrick M'Guire,	Same,	Land,	10 0 30	3 5 0	—	3 5 0
5 —	Bridget Burke,	Same,	Land,	18 3 34	4 15 0	—	4 15 0
			Total,	323 3 14	103 15 0	1 5 0	105 0 0
	CORRAWNAGH. (Ord. S. 81.)						
1 a	John Halligan,	Margaret M. Beaty,	Land, house, and offices,	14 2 0	3 0 0	0 5 0	3 5 0
2 a	Patrick Lyons,	Same,	Land, house, and offices,	13 1 15	3 0 0	0 5 0	3 5 0

A page from Griffith's Primary Valuation of Ireland showing some land and leaseholders in the parish of Aghamore.

reveal an area in which the name of interest is particularly common.

Further valuations of properties were conducted up to modern times . These can be inspected in "Cancellation Books" at the Valuation Office in Dublin. Copies of the primary valuations are in the Mayo County Library, NAI, National Library, Gilbert Library and most of the larger libraries. (See p. 58). A 'Full Name' index to Griffiths Valuations of Mayo has been published by Andrew J. Morris (U.S.). (See p. 86)

Registry of Deeds

A deed is a written witnessed agreement or undertaking by one or more parties. The vast majority deal with property transactions, e.g. leases, mortgages and conveyances. Business partnerships and marriage settlements were also registered. The Registry of Deeds was established in 1708 as a repository where deeds could be officially registered, but registration was not compulsory. The complete set of registered deeds is in the Registry of Deeds, Henrietta Street, Dublin. There are two sets of indexes which can be used to locate a deed, a Grantors Index and a Land Index.

Grantors Index: These are bound in volumes by initial letter of surname and a time-frame. e.g.: A 1708-1729.

The Grantor's name can be found alphabetically within each volume. The Grantor Index Books for the years 1708-1832 are arranged as follows: Surname and forename of grantor; surname (only) of grantee; & volume, page and number of the transcript. From 1833, the arrangement is as follows: Surname and forename of grantor; surname and forename of grantee; Location of land (not always stated); year of registration; & transcript volume and number.

Land Index: As there is no grantee index, and the researcher may not know the name of the grantor, the land indexes may be used. The Land Index Books are arranged by time frame for each county. The Land Index Books for Co. Mayo are as follows:

Time Frame	**Land Index Book Numbers**	
	Books arranged by barony	*Books indicating no barony*
1708-1738	38	-
1739-1810	39	-
1811-1820	40	-
1821-1825	41	-
1826-1828	42	-
1828-1832	116	-
1833-1835	153	173
1836-1839	202	220
1840-1844	248	269
1845-1849	298	318
1850-1854	348	369
1855-1859	398	419
1860-1861	444	444(also)
1862-1864	485	501
1865-1869	535	556
1870-1874	587 + 588	607
1875-1879	657 + 658	690

Time Frame	Land Index Book Numbers	
	Books arranged by barony	*Books indicating no barony*
1880-1884	730 + 731	763
1885-1889	803 + 804	836
1890-1894	880 + 881	902
1895-1899	946	975
1900-1904	1008	1026
1905-1909	1080	1104
1910-1914	1147	1169
1915-1919	1211	1229
1920-1929	1272 + 1273	1293
1930-1939	1324	1337
1940-1949	1363	1376

If the approximate date of a transaction is known, the relevant land index may be consulted. The Index is divided by barony. Within each barony the townlands are alphabetically arranged by first letter only. If the townland of interest is listed, the index will provide reference for all deeds which mention that townland or place. This is in the format 'Curhawnagh 1708 - 1832 Lyons to Waldron 23.345. 178034' (ie names of parties involved, and volume, page and transcript number). The details given from 1833 on are: land name, parish, name of grantor, name of grantee, year of registration, and volume, page and transcript numbers.

Some deeds were registered giving no indication of barony, so the 'no barony' books for the relative time-frame should be checked also.

Transcript Books: These contain verbatim transcripts of the original deeds. They are highly complex documents, hand-written and often difficult to read although the biographical information can usually be extracted without understanding the legal jargon.

Memorial: A memorial is the copy of the deed registered by the parties to the agreement or transaction. It is from this deed that the transcription is made. Photocopies of these can be obtained.

Abstract Books: These give details about the parties involved in agreements and transactions. There are no abstracts for the period 1708-1832.

Pre 1708 Deeds: A small collection of pre 1708 deeds for Mayo are held at the NAI. A card index is available, arranged by barony, giving the following details: Place, date, parties, nature of deed and reference number. The reference number may be used to obtain the deed required.

Encumbered Estates

Under the Encumbered Estates Act of 1849 the Encumbered Estates Court (later the Landed Estates Court) was established and empowered to sell or transfer the estates of insolvent or 'encumbered' owners.

Documents relating to the estates auctioned by the Encumbered Estates Court are held in the NAI, and the NLI. The O'Brien Rental Index, the Encumbered Estates Court Index to Conveyances, the Landed Estates Court Records of Conveyances and the Landed Estates Court Index can be consulted to obtain references for these records.

The Land Commission

The Land Commission was established in 1881, initially to arbitrate in claims of unfair rents made by tenants against their landlords. It also had the power to provide loans to tenants who wished to buy their land. Two card indexes (1) by estate (2) by vendor are available in the NLI. The Land Commission holds a much larger collection of land records, but these are not directly accessible for research. The Land Commission is housed in the same building as the NAI. A third card index to wills held by the Land Commission can also be consulted at the NLI.

Congested Districts Board

The Congested Districts Board was established in 1891. A congested district had a specific and complex definition, but was effectively a poor area with a high population which could not be economically sustained. The Board had responsibility for providing assistance to these districts, and to persons seeking relocation from these districts. They encouraged local industry and modernisation of farming. While the NAI hold some administration records, (reports were published) but the major records of transactions are held by the Land Commission (see above).

The Land Registry

In 1892 the Land registry was established to provide a system of compulsory registration of title of land bought under various land purchase acts. When title is registered all the relevant details are entered into numbered folios. The details in each folio are divided under the following headings: (i) Property location & barony (ii) Ownership (iii)Burdens.

Maps relating to all registrations are also held by the Land Registry. A folio can be located by a name index search (when the registered owner is known) or a map search (when the address is known). All title registrations for Mayo are held by the Land Registry, Setanta Centre, Dublin 2 and can be accessed by personal callers.

Estate Records

Estate records can sometimes provide the researcher with information about an ancestor who rented land from, or worked on, an estate. However, estate records are private and there is no central repository for those which are now on public access. They are in various national and local archives, and many still remain in private hands.

Estate records generally consist of any or all of the following: rentals, maps, deeds, wage books. To locate estate records, it is necessary to know the owner of the estate. This can be established by consulting one of the following:

(i) The lessor column of the Griffiths Valuations, although in many cases the lessor named is subletting from the estate owner.

(ii) The Land Owners of Ireland by U.H. Hussey deBurgh (1878).

(iii) The 'Persons' or 'Places' volume of Hayes' index to 'Manuscript Sources for the History of Irish Civilisation'. This gives a brief description of the type of records available within many major archives.

(iv) OS Fieldname books (see p.18 and 19)

Manuscript Sources for the History of Irish Civilisation

d Papers (from
Earl of Longford,
lating to the
ily of Cuffe of
lands in West-
Hibernica, No. 15,

e sales of Col.
Counties of Gal-
s of tenants, from

n.617 p.940

: Survey of the
ands in the Barony
of Borishoule,

Extracts mainly
Mayo from the
to the trustees
states.

Id. Ms. 14,405:
forfeited in 1688
drawn by J. Leigh,
ale 40 perches to
s "Trustees'

5 p.31

Deeds and convey-
Ireland, sold for
les Boyle, 3rd
6.

of A survey of
surveyed by F.
29 maps of South
egal action, in
), 1720-21.
nt, Balla, Co.

on the Cormick
perty of Mrs. M.
lane, Co. Cork,

Mayo, County: Estates:

Dublin: Public Record Office: M. 956, 958: Surveys of the estate of Thomas Ruttledge in the Barony of Kilmaine, Co. Mayo, 1749, 1770.

Mayo, County: Estates:

Winchester: Hampshire Record Office: Mss. 43 M. 48 (2665-2988): Papers of William Cope, silk manufacturer, of Dublin, including wills, legal and business papers, and estate papers relating to Dublin City, Mayo, Longford and Meath, 1750-1838. (For further details see Special List, No. 166).

Mayo, County: Estates:

Ms. 10,805: Blake Papers: State of the title of Sir Ulick Blake to his estates in Cos. Galway, Mayo and Clare, with some of his personal accounts, 1751-1754.

Mayo, County: Estates:

Manuscript map: Map of the demesne of Ballycally, situate in the barony of Carra, Co. Mayo. Traced for Mr. Randle McDonnell by John Adams. Vellum sheet, 27 by 14 inches, April, 1752.

16 I. 3 (15)

Mayo, County: Estates:

Winchester: Hampshire Record Office: Mss. 43 M. 48 (2611-2664): Personal, legal, and estate papers of Henry Cope (died 1815), including rentals, leases, etc. of estates in Mayo, Sligo and Westmeath, 1754-1811. (For further details, see Special List, No. 166).

Mayo, County: Estates:

Dublin: Public Record Office: M. 5527 (1-3): Judgment in Exchequer case, 1762, with fine of Curraghtown, Co. Meath, Mary Wood to Robert French, Justice of the Common Pleas, 1765 and constat of a decree of the Court of Claims assigning lands in Co. Mayo to Dominick French.

Mayo, County: Estates:

Belfast: Public Record Office: Microfilm 21: Correspondence and rent accounts of the Faulkner family relating to the bleaching business at Wellbrook, Co. Tyrone and the linen trade and to estates of which the Faulkners were agents, such as the Richardson estate, Coleraine, the Molesworth estate, Co. Mayo and the Whaley estate, Armagh, Dublin, Galway, 1764-1800.

Mayo, County: Estates:

Ainsworth (J. F.): Report on Mss.: other than

Mayo, County: Es

Ms. 5738: List
O'Donel's estate

Mayo, County: Es

Ms. 5821: Three
of the estates o
Mayo, together w
of the estates o
county submitted
Donel v. Medlico

Mayo, County: E

Manuscript map:
(Mweelis), Lecha
(Lisheenmanus) i
Mayo, part of th
veyed by John Ha
14 inches, colou

Mayo, County: E

Dublin: Public
M. 2250-61: T.
property of the
Queen's Co. but
Tyrone, Derry, a
iated families S
and Waring.

Mayo, County:

D. 15,409: Deed
Mayo, the Earl c
Bp. of Meath to

Mayo, County: E

Manuscript map:
ments at Moore H
seats of George
sheet, coloured,

Mayo, County:

Dublin: Public
Statements of t
premises in Newp
with genealogic
Laughlins and r
18th - 19th c.

Mayo, County:

Ms. 10,806: Bl
papers in legal
mainly involvin

A sample of entries from Haye's 'Manuscript Sources for the History of Irish Civilisation' showing some descriptions of Mayo estate records.

Chapter 9 Commercial & Social Directories

Directories were privately produced guides to traders and gentry in particular areas. They can provide valuable details about tradesmen, professionals, nobility and gentry, and occasionally about private residents and large farmers.

Both Pigot's and Slater's directories describe the towns and villages they include, noting churches, police stations, schools etc, and often naming public officials. Mayo towns are included in the following directories:

1784, '86 & 1803 -Wilson's Postchaise Companion

Describes 25 towns and villages of Mayo, noting local landmarks, public facilities and the seats (residences) of gentlemen and noblemen.

1812- Ambrose Leet's Directory

A directory of market towns, villages and other places noting prominent residents.

1814-Leet's Directory

As above with the addition of an index to persons. Also indexed in JNL.SMFHRL (1995) P. 34 - 54

1815- Further edition of Wilson's Post Chaise Companion - see above

1824-Pigot's City of Dublin & Hibernian Directory

Includes: Ballina, Ballinrobe, Castlebar, Killala, Swinford and Westport.

1846-Slaters National Commercial Directory of Ireland

Includes: Ballina, Ballinrobe, Castlebar, Claremorris, Killala, Newport, Swinford and Westport.

1856-Slaters Royal National Commercial Directory of Ireland

Includes: Ballina, Ballinrobe, Castlebar, Claremorris, Killala, Newport, Swinford and Westport.

1870-Slaters Directory of Ireland

Includes: Ballina, Ballinrobe, Hollymount, Castlebar, Claremorris, Ballyhaunis, Killala, Newport, Swinford & Foxford and Westport.

1881- Slaters Royal National Commercial Directory of Ireland

Includes: Ballina, Ballinrobe & Hollymount, Castlebar, Claremorris, Ballyhaunis & Knock, Newport & neighbourhood, Swinford & Foxford and Westport.

1894-Slaters Royal National Directory of Ireland

Covers all Mayo parishes, and major towns and villages.

Wilson's Postchaise Companion and Leet's Directories can be found in the NLI (J 9141 W13 & Ir. 9141 L10 respectively). Both Pigot's and Slater's Directories are in the NLI and the Gilbert Library, and in other major libraries.

Mayo Towns included in Commercial Directories:

Towns	**Pigot's**	**Slater's**				
	1824	1846	1856	1870	1881	1894
Ballina						●
Ballinrobe						●
Ballyhaunis	●	●	●			●
Castlebar						●
Claremorris	●					●
Foxford	●	●	●			●
Hollymount	●	●	●			●
Killala					●	●
Knock	●	●	●	●		●
Newport	●					●
Swinford						●
Westport						●
All Civil Parishes						●

Chapter 10 Newspapers

Some 24 newspapers published in, or pertaining to, Mayo survive for the period 1812 to date. The information in newspapers varies from birth, marriage and death notices to business notices. Although the main interest to genealogists is the notices of births, deaths and marriages, these notices mainly refer to wealthier families. Newspapers can, however, provide excellent details of everything from accidents to court proceedings. It was a common practice for newspapers to publish a list of all those who perished in a boating accident and also to print the details of those who appeared at the local assizes.

Articles submitted by private individuals are also found in local newspapers and these give an insight to Mayo life at that period. The surviving newspapers for Co. Mayo are at the NLI, the British Library (BL) and Mayo Co. Library (MCL), although some of these collections are incomplete. Photocopies are usually available for a fee.

Title: **Aegis & Western Courier** (Castlebar)
Published: 6.1841-11.1842
Holdings: NLI: 6.1841-11.1842. mf.
BL: 6.1841-11.1842, Hard copy & mf.
NLI: 6.1841-11.1842. mf.
MCL: 6.1841-11.1842 mf.

Title: **Ballina Advertiser, Mayo & Sligo Commercial Gazette**
Published: 1.1840- 11.1843.
Holdings: NLI: 1.1840-11.1843 mf.
BL.1.1840-11.1843 Hard copy & mf.
MCL: 1.1840-11.1843 mf.

Title: **Ballina Chronicle**
Published: 5.1849-8.1851, Incorp. with Connaught Watchman.
Holdings: BL. 5.1849-8.1851 mf. & Hard copy
MCL: 5.1849-8.1851 mf.

Title: **Ballina Herald**
Published: 1844-1891, cont. as Ballina Herald & Mayo & Sligo Advertiser 1891-4.1962. Incorp. with Western People
Holdings: NLI: 8.1927-4.1962 mf.
BL: 10.1891-11.1892, 4.1913-1924, 1926-1929, 1931-4.1962 Hard copy.1.-7, & 9.-11.1892 mf.
MCL: 10.1891-7.1892; 9.1892-11. 1892;4.1913-6.1922; 8.1922-12.1924; 1.1926-4.1962 mf.

Title: **Ballina Impartial** or **Tyrawley Advertiser**
Published: 1.1823-11.1835
Holdings: NLI: 1.1823-1825; 1827-11.1835 mf.
BL: 1.1823-1825; 1.1827-11.1835 Hard copy & mf.
MCL: 1.1823-11.1835 mf.

Title: **Ballina Journal & Connaught Advertiser**
Published: Circa.1880- 3.1895
Holdings: BL: 11.1882-3.1895 Hard copy & mf.
NLI: 11.1882-3.1895 mf.

Title: **Ballinrobe Chronicle & Mayo Advertiser**
Published: 9.1866-12.1867; 4.1868-10.1903
Holdings: NLI: 9.1866-12.1867, 4.1868-10.1903 mf.
BL: 9.1866-12.1867, 4.1868-10.1903 Hard copy & mf.
MCL: 9.1866-10.1903 mf.

Title: **Connaught Telegraph** (Castlebar) ***see Telegraph***

Title: **Connaught Ranger** ***see Telegraph***

Title: **Connaught Watchman** (Ballina)
Published: 8.1851-10.1863
Holdings: BL: 8.1851-10.1863 Hard copy
8.1851-1859; 1862-10.1863 mf.
MCL: 8.1851-10.1863 mf.

Title: **Galway Express, Mayo, Roscommon, Clare & Limerick Advertiser**
Published: 1.1853-9.1920
Holdings: NLI: 1885-9.1917 Hard copy
1853-9.1920 mf. (Except the above)
BL: 1.1853-1855, 2.1856-1918, 4.1919-9.1920 Hard copy & mf.
BELB: 1885-9.1920 mf.

Title: **Galway, Mayo, Roscommon, Sligo & Clare Chronicle** ***see Irishman***

Title: **Irishman** or **Galway, Mayo, Roscommon, Sligo & Clare Chronicle**
Published: 5-12.1835
Holdings: NLI: 5-12.1835 mf.
BL: 5-12.1835 Hard copy & mf.

Title: **Mayo Constitution** (Castlebar)
Published: Circa 5.1805- 5.1872
Holdings: NLI: 1853-11.1871 Hard copy.1812*; 1828-1852 mf.
BL: 12.1812*; 1828-11.1871;4.1872*-5.1872* Hard copy & mf.
MCL: 1.1828-11.1871 mf. (* Single issues only)

Title: **Mayo Examiner & West of Ireland Agriculture & Commercial Reporter & Advertiser** (Castlebar)
Published: 7.1868-6.1903
Holdings: BL: 7.1868-6.1903 (Hard copy) 7.1868-1882; 1884; 1886-1896 (Mf.)
MCL: 7.1868-6.1903 mf.
SOG: 1877-1883 mf.

Title: **Mayoman** (Castlebar)
Published: 5.1919-10.1920, 2.-6.1921
Holdings: NLI: 6.1919-10.1920, 2.1921-6.1921 mf., Imperfect
BL: 5.1919-10.1920, 2.1921-6.1921 Hard copy
MCL: 6.1919-10.1920; 2. -6.1921 mf.

Title: **Mayo Mercury & Connaught Advertiser** (Castlebar)
Published: 1.1840-3.1841
Holdings: NLI: 1.1840-3.1841 mf.
BL: 1.1840-3.1841 mf. & Hard copy
MCL: 1.1840-3.1841 mf.

Title: **Mayo News** (Westport)
Published: Circa 11.1892 to date.
Holdings: NLI: 6.1921-1976 (Hard copy) 1977 -1981 mf.
1982-in progress (Hard copy); 1893-1981 mf.
BL: 1.1893-12.1922.1924- to date. (Hard copy).1893-1976 mf.
MCL: 1.1893 to date. mf.

Title: **Mayo & Sligo Intelligencer** ***see Tyrawly Herald***

Title: **Telegraph** or **Connaught Ranger** (Castlebar)
Published: 1828-1870; 1876-date (as Connaught Telegraph)
Holdings: NLI: 9.1830-8.1870 mf.; 6.1879-12.1913. 6.1919-12.1974 (Hard copy)
1975 in progress mf.
BL: 9.1830-12.1855, 2.1856-11.1856, 2. -8.1870; 5. 1876
Hard copy 1876 - 1974 MF.
also: 15.12.1869, 12 & 19.1 1870 Hard copy. 9.1830-8.1870 mf.
SOG: 1836-1838 mf.
MCL: 9.1830-8.1870;5.1876 mf.
SMFHRC: Index to all persons listed, 1828-1900

Title: **Tyrawly Herald** or **Mayo & Sligo Intelligencer** (Ballina)
Published: 1844-1870
Holdings: NLI: : 1.1844-12.1860, 1.1861-9.1870 mf.
BL: 1.1844-12.1860, 1.1861-9.1870 mf. & Hard copy
MCL: : 1.1844-9.1870 mf.

Title: **Western Gem** (Ballina)
Published: 1843
Holdings: NLI: 4.1843-12.1843 mf.
BL: None Held
MCL: 4.1843-12.1843 mf.

Title: **Western Nationalist, Roscommon, Mayo, Leitrim & Sligo News** (Boyle)
Published: 1907-1920
Holdings: NLI: 3.1907-4.1920 mf.
BL: 3.1907-4.1920 mf. & Hard copy

Title: **Western People** (Ballina)
Published: 1883-to date
Holdings: NLI: 1914-1982 Hard copy. 5.1889-12.1913; 1983-in progress mf.
BL: 5.1889-12.1929; 1931-Hard copy. 5.1889-12.1976 mf.
MCL: 5.1889-mf.

Title: **Western Star** (Ballina)
Published: 1835-1837
Holdings: BL: 12.1835-5.1837 Hard copy

Chapter 11 Family Names and Histories

Family Names

To indicate the range and extent of various surnames in Co. Mayo, a table of the 20 most common names was compiled from the parish surname indexes of Griffiths Valuation Survey (1855/57). It includes surnames of those which occurred 10 or more times in each civil parish. Where no surname numbering 10 or more occurred in a parish, the most numerous surname was included. The table below lists the 20 most numerous surnames, indicating where they are most common.

Surname	*Total No.*	*No. of Parishes*	*Parishes with most occurrences (& No.)*	*Barony with most occurrences (& No.)*
Walsh	822	37	Killedan (64)	Carra (193)
Gallagher	468	14	Kilbeagh (99)	Gallen (155)
Kelly	370	25	Kilbeagh (32)	Costello (84)
Moran	356	19	Burrishoole (38)	Burrishoole (83)
Malley/O'Malley	296	9	Kilgeever (114)	Murrisk (191)
Burke/Bourke	251	17	Oughaval (30)	Kilmaine (53)
Duffy	226	7	Kilmovee (88)	Costello (182)
Durkan/Durkin	199	5	Kilconduff (67)	Gallen (179)
Murphy	194	12	Kilcommon-Erris (46)	Costello (49)
Barrett	189	8	Kilmore (54)	Erris (104)
Gibbons	185	11	Ballyovey (31)	Burrishoole (69)
McHale	170	7	Turlough (63)	Tyrawley (97)
McDonnell	153	10	Kilcommon-Erris (26)	Tyrawley (49)
Lyons	137	4	Annagh (48)	Costelloe (132)
Ruane	125	7	Kilgarvan (34)	Gallen (89)
Brennan	123	6	Killedan (45)	Gallen (73)
McNulty	117	4	Killasser (69)	Gallen (103)
Gaughan	112	3	Kilcommon-Erris (64)	Erris (91)
McNicholas	108	4	Bohola (48)	Gallen (108)
O'Donnell	106	7	Castlemore (22)	Erris/Burrishoole (28)

Published Family Histories

A large selection of family histories and pedigrees have been published both independently and in the journals of local history and genealogical societies. These are very predominantly for the wealthier families. They are:

Family	*Location*	*Source*
Bellew	Castlebar	Irish & Anglo Irish Gentry p. 195- (1884, Dublin)
Bingham	Bingham Castle	Visitation of Ireland Vol. 5 (1911, Privately Pub.)
Boyd	Mayo	Burke's Col. Gentry p. 511-
Brewster	Mayo	J. SMFHRC (1995) p. 20-
Browne	Breaffy	Burke's Irish Family Records p. 173- (1976, London)
Browne	Westport House	D. Browne (1981) (a)
Burke	Mayo	RIA M1001
Dolan	Pulbawn	J. SMFHRC (1994) p. 62-
Elwood	Mayo	Ir. Gen. Vol. 6 (4) (1983) p. 477-
Fair	Levally, Ballinrobe	J. SMFHRC (1996) p. 43-
Fitzgerald	Mayo	Burke's Irish Family Records p. 420- (1976, London)
Gray	Claremorris	Ir. Gen. Vol. 7 (4) (1989) p. 551-
Heaney	S.E. Mayo Sept.	J. SMFHRC (1990) p. 32-
Judge	Claremorris	J. SMFHRC (1995) p. 9-
Kelly	Westport	Fr. Vincent Kelly (1995) (b)
Lambert	Brookhill	Ir. Gen. Vol. 3 (10) (1965) p. 372-
Livingston	Westport	J. SMFHRC (1995) p. 55-
MacDonald	Mayo	J. Galway Arch. Hist. Soc. 17. (1936-37) p. 65
McHale	Tubbernavine, Addergoole.	Irish & Anglo-Irish Gentry p. 106- (1884, Dublin)
Mellett	Sept of S. Mayo	J. SMFHRC (1996) p. 22-
Moore	Ballina	Irish & Anglo-Irish Gentry p. 221 (1884, Dublin)
Moore	Moorehall	JRSAI 36 (1906) p. 224-
Morris	Mayo	E. Naomi Chapman (1928) (c)
Nally	Balla	J. SMFHRC (1992) p. 52-
Nally	Currantawy & Castlelucas	J. SMFHRC (1993) p. 23-
O'Malley	Mayo	Anal. Hib. 25. p. 185-
O'Malley	Mayo (1651-1725)	J. Galway Arch Hist. Soc. 25 (1) (1952) p. 32-
Ormsby	Tobervaddy	Ir. Gen. Vol. 1(9) (1941) p. 284-
Ruttledge	Mayo	Ir. Gen. Vol. 7(3) (1988) p. 433-
Ruttledge	Mayo	Burke's Irish Family Records p. 999- (1976, London)
Tighe	Ballinrobe/Crossboyne	J. SMFHRC (1992) p. 39-
Treston	Mayo	J. SMFHRC (1991) p. 57-

(a) Westport House and the Brownes
(b) Biography of Patrick Joseph and Kathleen Kelly, Westport, Co. Mayo.
(c) Memoirs of my family, together with some researchers into the early history of the Morris families of Tipperary, Galway and Mayo.

Related Papers

Manuscripts and typescripts relating to Irish families can be found in various Irish repositories. The content of these papers includes genealogies, histories, deeds, obituaries and copies of early census returns. The following is a list relating to Mayo families, indicating family history relevance:

Bingham: (née **Cuffe**) Communion Prayers of Jane, Lady Bingham with a list of family obituaries. [17th century] T.C.C. Ms. 4460 (E.6.15)

Blake: 11 deeds relating to Blake properties outside the Barony of Carra, 1688-1855. NLI D.16, 888-98.

Blake: Blake family papers including a Connaught Certificate, Decree of Innocence and Inquisitions etc. [17th & 18th century] NAI .

Blake: Glynn Notebook (No. 62), Notes by John Glynn on Blake in Galway & Mayo. [19th century] NLI Ms. 7928

Blake: 41 Deeds relating to Blake properties (Barony of Carra) 1772-1863. NLI, D. 16, 847-87.

Browne: Papers and Deeds of Browne Family of Co. Mayo [Sligo Papers] NLI pos. 940

Curry: Copies of census returns of Curry family of Mayo 1851. NAI . M.5249 (14)

Daly: Notebook of Patrick Daly, Shrule, Co. Mayo who emigrated to America and settled in San Francisco. Included genealogical notes relating to the Daly family. [1854-1942] PRONI mic. 179

Egan: Copies of census returns of Egan family of Mayo 1851 NAI . M. 5249(22)

Egan: A short account of the Egan family of Castlebar in the form of a letter from John Egan to his son Joseph Bernard. [Nov. 13, 1905] NLI pos.4910

Glendenning: Papers relating to the Glendenning family of Mayo. NAI M. 1043-7, T.3871

Greal: 1821 Census return of James Greal and family of Kilbelfad. NAI . M. 151

Higgins: Genealogical notes on the Higgins family of Mayo. [c. 1750-1872] PRONI T. 481

Lynch: Copies of census returns of Lynch family of Mayo 1821. NAI . M. 5246 (7)

McCostello: Genealogical notes on Angulo or McCostello family Co. Mayo. [1172-1780] P.R.O.N.I.

McGuire: Copies of census returns of McGuire family of Mayo 1841.
NAI . M. 5248 (11)

Mullaney: Copies of census returns of Mullaney family of Mayo 1841.
NAI . M. 5248 (15)

O'Donel: Inscriptions at the O'Donel family vault, Straide Abbey.
(9 documents) [c. 1896] NLI Pos. 4160.

O'Malley: History and genealogy of the O'Malley family of Co. Mayo [1688-1823] (1,000+ documents). NLI Mss. 8204-8214. Detailed hand-list. Pos. 2935

O'Malley: History of Belclare Branch of O'Malley family (17th & 18th c.) by Sir Owen O'Malley. Reprinted in J. Galway Arch.Hist. Soc.1950-1952.
NLI Ms. 5619 also M. 5620 for the period 1820-1860.

Phillips: Copies of census returns of Phillips of Mayo 1841
NAI M. 5248 (18)

Chapter 12. Gravestone Inscriptions

As the civil registration of deaths in Ireland only commenced in 1864, and few churches kept burial records, gravestones provide one of the very few pre-1864 sources of information about date and place of death. However, gravestones can also provide many other items of information of great value to the researcher.

Many gravestones provide only basic details i.e. the name of the deceased and the date of death. However, some are more detailed, and provide excellent biographical details about the deceased, and about other relatives not previously known. The graves of poorer persons, unfortunately, were often unmarked, or marked with wooden memorials. Gravestones are therefore not a source that can be expected for poorer ancestors

It should be remembered that Catholics, Methodists and Presbyterians have at all times been buried in Church of Ireland graveyards. CoI graveyard and burial records should therefore always be checked, whatever the denomination of the family.

The information on Gravestone inscriptions and other memorials have been transcribed and published in many sources down through the years. Among the most notable of the groups involved was the Association for the Preservation of the Memorials of the Dead (1888-1921) whose members and supporters transcribed records from hundreds of sites around Ireland. These were published in the Journal of the Association (JAPMD). The society was continued as the Irish Memorials Association after 1922. The memorials published by the JAPMD were selective, since they were generally dependent on contributions by individual members. In many cases transcriptions from a specific graveyard were published a couple at a time over several years in various volumes which in many cases did not accumulate to provide a full set of transcripts. (see p. 75).

There are over 120 graveyards in Co. Mayo of which only a fraction have been transcribed and published in some form to date. A full list of Mayo burial grounds and their caretakers can be obtained by writing to: Mayo County Council, Aras an Chontae, Castlebar, Co. Mayo. In recent years local genealogical and historical societies have been transcribing and publishing complete surveys of these graveyards. This has now become a common practice and local journals should be continually checked for new additions. In Mayo, the SMFHRC has been actively abstracting and publishing this information for years.

The inscriptions published to date by the JAPMD or the SMFHRC are:

Journal of the Association for the Preservation of the Memorials of the Dead in Ireland:

Aughaval	Vol. I No. 3	(1890)	p. 221
Balla Holy Well	Vol. X No. 6	(1920)	p. 367
Ballinasmala Abbey	Vol. V No. 3(2)	(1903)	p. 408
Ballinrobe Parish Church	Vol. IV No. 2	(1899)	p. 283-84

Also:	Vol. V, No. 1(2)	(1901)	p. 93-94
	Vol. V No. 3(2)	(1903)	p. 405-407
	Vol. VI No. 1(2)	(1904)	p. 121
	Vol. VII No. 1	(1907)	p. 151-152
Ballycastle Churchyard	Vol. VIII No. 6	(1912)	p. 603-604
Ballyglass Wayside Monument	Vol. IX No. 6	(1916)	p. 539
Ballyovey see Partry			
Burrishoole Abbey	Vol. 1 No. 4	(1891)	p. 452
Also:	Vol. VI No. 3 (2)	(1906)	p. 588
Burrishoole, Newport Church	Vol. I No. 4	(1891)	p. 452-455
Castlebar Old Graveyard	Vol. VIII No. 4	(1911)	p. 399
Cloonlagheen see Partry			
Cong Abbey	Vol. II No. 2	(1893)	p. 334-337
Also:	Vol. II No. 3	(1894)	p. 526-528
Crossboyne Churchyard	Vol. IX No. 2	(1914)	p.136-139
Also see Ballyglass			
Doonfeeney Churchyard	Vol. VIII No. 6	(1912)	p. 604
Doonfeeney see also Ballycastle			
Hollymount Churchyard	Vol. VII No. 2	(1908)	p. 415-418
Kilcolman see Ballinasmala			
Kilcommon see Hollymount			
Kilkerrin Churchyard	Vol. IX No. 4	(1915)	p. 336
Kilmaine Parish Church	Vol. IV No. 3(2)	(1900)	p. 447-451
Killala, St. Patricks Cathedral	Vol. I No. 4	(1891)	p. 455-456
Also:	Vol. IV No. 2	(1899)	p. 280-282
Killedan Church	Vol IV No. 1	(1898)	p. 105-108
Also:	Vol. VIII No. 2	(1910)	p. 129-130
Also:	Vol. VIII No. 4	(1911)	p. 399
Kilmolara see Neale			
Murrisk Abbey	Vol. III No. 2	(1896)	p. 322
Neale Park Monument	Vol. VII No. 3	(1909)	p. 638-645
Newport see Burrishoole			
Partry Private Cemetery	Vol. VIII No. 2	(1910)	p. 130-134
Turlough Churchyard	Vol. VIII No. 4	(1911)	p. 399-400
Urlare Abbey	Vol. I No. 4	(1891)	p. 456-457
Westport see Aughaval			

Journal of the Irish Memorials Association:

Castlebar Parish Church	Vol. XI No. 3	(1922)	p. 217-218
Killala Cathedral	Vol. XI No. 5	(1924)	p. 310

Gravestone Inscriptions Published by South Mayo Family History Research Centre:

Balla & Mayo Abbey CoI Graveyards- JSMFHRC 1988
Ballinchalla Cemetery (pre 1900) JSMFHRC 1990
Ballynew Cemetery- JSMFHRC 1991
Castlebar Cemetery (pre-1800) JSMFHRC 1992
Castlebar: Gravestone Inscriptions from South Mayo: Vol. 1 (Mayo, SMFHRC 1995)
Claremorris RC Church- JSMFHRC 1993
Hollymount see Kilcommon

Islandeady: Gravestone Inscriptions from South Mayo: Vol. 1 (Mayo, SMFHRC 1995)
Kilcommon Cemetery, Hollymount, 18th century- JSMFHRC 1989
Kilfraughans Cemetery- JSMFHRC 1992
Kilgeever: Gravestone Inscriptions from South Mayo: Vol. 2 (Mayo, SMFHRC ; In press)
Killedan CoI Churchyard- JSMFHRC 1989
Killedan Cemetery- JSMFHRC 1992
Kilmeena CoI Churchyard- JSMFHRC 1993
Kilmeena: Gravestone Inscriptions from South Mayo: Vol. 2 (Mayo, SMFHRC ; In press)
Mayo Abbey see Balla
Moyne Cemetery- JSMFHRC 1992
Oughaval: Gravestone Inscriptions from South Mayo: Vol. 2 (Mayo, SMFHRC ; In press)

Killedan Church.

[From Mr. George Ormsby.]

'The inscription which is given below is copied from a slab now fixed into the wall of the church porch at Killedan; it was originally built into the gable of the ruined church of Loughkeeaune (?), some miles to the north-east of Killedan, but had fallen out, and was lying on the ground in two pieces, having evidently been broken by the fall. The cut-stone moulding in which the stone had been set remained in position in the gable wall of the church, the ruins of which and its surrounding burial-ground are situated in the middle of a field, and open to the trespass of cattle; in order to preserve the stone, it was removed, and erected in its present position in the porch of Killedan church some years ago.

'This stone is a large slab of limestone, about four feet by five feet, and about four inches thick. The coats-of-arms and inscription are carved in relief. The E at the beginning of ERECTED, at the end of the inscription, was accidentally omitted, and had to be afterwards inserted. Owing to the break in the stone, the letters at the beginning of the inscription are damaged; the latter runs thus':—

HERE LYES INTERRED THE BODY OF ROBERT
ORMSBY ESQR LATE OF REDHILL WHO
DEPARTED THIS LIFE THE 28TH OF DECE-
MBER 1727 AND IN Y^{E} 61ST YEAR OF HIS
AGE. TO HIS MEMORY HIS LATE FAITH-
FVL AND AFFECTIONATE CONSORT ELIZA-
BETH ORMSBY ALIAS KELLY HAS CAVS-
ED THIS MONVMENT TO BE$_{E}$RECTED:

'The coats-of-arms at the top of the stone are those of Ormsby and of O'Kelly.

Page from 'J Association for Preservation of Memorials of the Dead' (1910)

CONVERT ROLLS

Gilday, Peter, cert. 2 March 1789, enrolled 13 May 1789 (A).

Gildea, George, Co Mayo, gent., cert. 8 March 1719, enrolled 15 March 1719 (A). Conformity 2 November 1718 (B). Enrolled 5 June 1723 [Probable confusion with James Gildea] (C).

Gildea, James, Dublin, cert. and enrolled 5 June 1723 (A). Conformity 5 June 1723 (B). Enrolled 15 March 1719 [Probable confusion with George Gildea] (C).

Gildea, James, Island Bridge, Co Dublin, cert. 23 October 1733, enrolled 23 October 1753 (A). Conformity and cert. 23 October 1753 (B).

Gildea, James, senior, Drum, Co Mayo, cert. 3 May 1762, enrolled 7 May 1762 (A). Gildea, James, the elder, now of Drum, conformity "several yrs since", enrollment 7 June 1762 (B). Gent., of Weatherford, p. Drum (D).

Giles, otherwise Bourke, Honor, of Cargin, cert. 25 February 1787, enrolled 16 December 1788 (A).

Gillaspy, Andrew, Castlepollard, cert. 10 June 1774, enrolled 30 July 1774 (A).

Gillaspy, Martha, Castlepollard, cert. 10 June 1774, enrolled 30 July 1774 (B).

Gillett, Peter, cert. 4 June 1787, enrolled 30 June 1787 (A).

Gillfoyle, William, farmer, Lismacken, Co Tipperary, cert. 8 July 1765, enrolled 10 July 1765 (A). Conformity 7 July 1765 (B).

Gillmer, Alice, cert. 11 December 1773, enrolled 24 December 1773 (A).

Gilmore, Morgan, Ballinthalla, Co Mayo, cert. 25 December 1760, enrolled 21 January 1761 (A). P. Ballinchalla, conformity 21 December 1760 (B). (D).

Gilsenan, Richard, Dublin, cert. and enrolled 17 January 1748 (A). Conformity 15 January 1748 (B).

Giraghty, James, Eyrecourt, Co Galway, cert. 31 April 1741, enrolled 23 December 1741 (A). Conformity 30 January 1740 (B).

Giraghty, Margaret, cert. 30 March 1783, enrolled 3 May 1783 (A).

Giraghty, Thomas, Roscommon, cert. 19 June 1732, enrolled 22 June 1723 (A). Giraghty, Mr Thomas, p. Roscommon, conformity 29 October 1721 (B). Geraghty, Mr Thomas, enrolled 20 June 1723 (C).

Giraghty, Thomas, d. Elphin, cert. 2 March 1724, enrolled 5 March 1724 (A). Conformity 27 February 1724 (B). (C). Gent. (D).

Giree, Wm., cert. 17 April 1768, enrolled 22 April 1768 (A). Geeree, William, p. Clonmel, Co Tipperary, conformity 1 November 1767 (B).

Glaney, William, Dublin, cert. 15 September 1766, enrolled 18 September 1766 (A). Now of Dublin, conformity 12 September 1766 (B).

Glascock, Alice, Dublin, cert. 24 May 1762, enrolled 25 May 1762 (A). Conformity 23 May 1762 [bracketed with Silvester Glascock] (B).

Glascock, Ellinor, of Thurles, cert. 8 April 1788, enrolled 6 April 1788 (A).

A page from the Convert Rolls
Edited by Eileen O'Byrne (IMC 1981)

Chapter 13 Mayo in 1798

One of the most notable events in the history of Mayo was the landing of the French at Killala in August 1798. Although all previous rebellions in other parts of the country in May and June of 1798 were crushed, the landing of General Humbert and his men gave new hope. This hope was dashed after less than a month when General Humbert and his men were halted in their tracks at Ballinamuck, Co. Longford. The accounts of this conflict, and the land confiscations and other reprisals which followed, can provide useful background information, and specific family details of Mayo people of the period. Some relevant sources are listed below.

Year of the French, Thomas Flanagan. Publ: H. Holt & Co., 1989 USA.

Narrative of events in Co. Mayo during the insurrection of 1798 in which James McDonald an uncle of the author took part. NLI Ms. 7335.

Incomplete letter addressed to 'My Dear Aunt' written from Castlebar, Co. Mayo, October 1798. Giving an account of events connected with the Rising. NLI Ms. 8283

Rev. James Little's Diary of the French landing in 1798. Edited by Nuala Costello. R.I.A. Ms. 3.B.51. Also Analecta Hib. No. 11. 1941.

Letter of Catherine Carroll to her mother, giving an account of the 1798 rebellion in which her uncle was in the English cavalry. Hollymount, May 29, 1798. DOD Ms. Also Hist. Mss. Comm. Report 3 App. 1872 p. 260.

Dilemma at Killala, 1798 Irish Sword Vol. 8, No. 33 (1968) p. 261-273

The Battle of Castlebar, 1798 Irish Sword Vol. 3 No. 11 (1957) p. 107-114

Diary of Dr. Joseph Stock, Bishop of Killala from August 23-September 20 1798. T.C.D. Ms. 1690 (s.3.17)

Letters from Lady Anne Mahon, Dublin and Westport, Co. Mayo to her daughter the Hon. Mrs Anne Browne in Ayr (Scotland) 1798 concerning the Rebellion in Mayo. PRONI T. 2626

Copy, Proclamation of James McDonnell Carnacon, Co. Mayo 1798 and letters from him in America 1798-1837. NAI . 999/49

Diary of Captain Joseph Bull-Irish Sword Vol. 8 No. 30 + 31 (1967); Vol. 8 (32) & (33) (1968)

The Last Invasion of Ireland by Richard Hayes (Dublin, 1939). (see below).

5 Letters of the Marquis of Buckingham to Lord Grenville giving details of the campaign in Co. Mayo and elsewhere and debates in the Dublin parliament. Fortescue Mss. Also Hist. Mss. Comm. Report. Fortescue Ms. V4 1905 p. 286-293

Prince of Wales Pay-book, indexed by surname giving details of subsistence, rations, stoppages etc. NLI Ms. 11,880.

An article on the French in Killala in 1798 (McGarrity Papers) NLI Ms. 17;559

The Government Forces Engaged off Castlebar in 1798 by Sir Henry McAnally.
Irish Hist. Studies, Vol. IV No. 16 Sept 1945, p. 316-331.

NAI Rebellion Papers: An indexed collection of rebellion papers are held at the NAI. A small amount of these papers refer to Mayo and can be inspected in the reading room.

PROSCRIPTIONS AND BANISHMENTS 181

hension or for such private information as may cause to be apprehended any and each of the other persons undernamed:

James Joseph McDonnell of Carnacon.
Christopher Crump, Esq., M.D., of Oury.
Valentine Jordan, Esq., of Forkfield.
Mr. John Gibbons of Westport.
Rev. Myles Prendergast, Friar, of Westport.
Rev. Michael Gannon of Louisburgh, Priest.
Rev. Manus Sweeney of Newport, Priest.
Mr. Peter Gibbons of Newport, Merchant.
James McDonnell, Esq., of Newport.
Thomas Gibbons of Croc, Farmer.
Austin O'Malley of Borrisool.
Thomas Fergus of Murrisk, Farmer.
James McGreal of Kilguever.
Hugh McGuire of Crossmolina, Farmer.
Edmond McGuire of Crossmolina.
Hugh McGuire, junr., of Crossmolina.
Patrick Barrett of the town of Ballina, Yeoman.
Michael Canavan of the town of Ballina, Painter.
Thomas Rigney of Ballymanagh.
Pat McHale of Crossmolina, Farmer.
James Toole, late of Co. Armagh.
Pat Loughny of Raheskin, Farmer.
Martin Harkan of Cloongullane.
John Heuston of Castlebar, Chandler."

The list is far from being a complete one of the Irish leaders outlawed, those cited in it being representatives only of the northern and western districts of Mayo. Most of them have already been met casually in the course of this narrative, and it would be well, perhaps, to give a fuller account of them and of their subsequent fortunes.

Among those proscribed, as may be seen, were several members of the Gibbons clan, which was widely spread

A page from 'The Last Invasion of Ireland' by Richard Hayes describing the 1798 Rebellion

Chapter 14 Further Reading:

Further Reading

Shipwrecks Off The Irish Coast 1105-1993. Edward J. Burke
This book gives accounts of 71 shipwrecks and sinkings pertaining to Mayo. (Dublin 1994)

Mayo Places, their Names and Origins. Nollaig O'Muraile (Pub F.N.T. Dublin 1985)

Claremorris in History
Ed. Marie Mahon (1987)-[Mayo Family Hist. Soc. 1987]

Notes on Cong and the Neale by Rev. John Neary P.P. (Dundalk; Dundalgan Press; 1938)

Achill by Kenneth McNally (David and Charles, Newtonabbot 1973)

The Surnames of Crossmolina
by Bridie Greavy-Mayo Nth. Heritage Centre J. 1995. p. 6-19.

The Surnames of Kilcolman from Marriage Records of the Last Century
by Damien McGahon - 'Claremorris in History' (1987)

Achill Island-Archaeology, History and Folklore
by Theresa McDonald (I.A.S. 1997)

A Short History of Ballymackeehola Townland (Ballysakeery Parish)
J. Nth. Mayo Hist.& Arch Soc.. Vol. 1 (3) 1985 p. 40-44

History of Mayo (Transcript copies)
by Rev. Michael O'Flannagan NLI Ms. 5133-38

History of Ballinrobe
by H. Knox, NLI Ms. 2061

Notes on the Early History of the Dioceses of Tuam, Killala and Achonry
by Herbert Thomas Knox (Dublin 1904)

Erris in the Irish Highlands and the Atlantic Railway
by P. Knight (Dublin 1836)

Ordnance Survey Letters, Co. Mayo
Letters relating to the antiquities of the County of Mayo containing information collected during the progress of the Ordnance Survey in 1838. 2 volumes published in 1926 NLI Ir. 9141 014

A deBurgo Silver Chalice, A.D. 1494 (with notes on the family of Bourke of Turlough) - Galway Arch. and Hist. Soc. J. Vol. 5 (4) (1908) p. 241-245

A Map of Part of County Mayo in 1584 (with notes and an account of its author John Browne of the Neale) Galway Arch and Hist. Soc. J. Vol. 5. (3) (1908) p. 145-158.

A Short History of Ballinrobe Parish. Rev. M. Dalton (Dublin, Browne & Nolan, 1931)

Burrishoole Abbey Rev. M. O'Donnell (Dublin 1929)

Chieftain to Knight-Tibbutt Bourke 1567-1629, First Viscount Mayo.
Anne Chambers (Dublin, Wolfhound Press, 1983)

Crossmolina-An Historical Survey.
Crossmolina Hist. & Arch. Soc.

17th Century Documents Relating to the Manors of Aughrim and Burrishoole
Galway Arch. and Hist. Soc. J. Vol. 16 (1934) p. 48-56

Evictions of the Lucan Estate, Ballinrobe 1848
J. SMFHRC (1995) p. 59-69

Families of Ballycroy Parish, 1856-1880
William G. Masterson (Indianapolis 1995)

Granuaile-The Life and Times of Grace O'Malley c. 1530-1603.
Anne Chambers (Dublin, Wolfhound Press, 1988)

History of Ballybrooney Townland (Ballysakeery)
J. Nth Mayo Hist, and Arch., Soc. (1995/6) p. 30-40

History of Inishboffin and Innishark
Irish Ecclesiastical Record Vol. 16 (1920) p. 216-228

History of Mayo
J.F. Quinn (Originally published in the form of weekly articles in the Western People, Ballina in the 1930's. Three volumes published since 1993).

Itchy Feet and Thirsty Work - A Guide to the History and Folklore of Ballinrobe.
Bridie Mulloy (Ballinrobe 1991)

Killala Diocese 1830-45 (Nth Mayo Hist. & Arch. Journal Vol. 1 (1-4) 1982-86)

Killasser, A History
B. O'Hara (1981)

Land Ownership in the Barony of Costello 1635
J. SMFHRC (1996) p. 55-68

Mayo 5000, Heritage of Mayo
Aine Ni Cheannain (1982)

Mayo Abbey: The Diocese and Abbey of Mayo
William H. Gratten-Irish Ecclesiastical Record, Vol. 21, June 1907, p. 603-609

Mayo Landholders in the 17th Century.
J. RSAI Vol. 95 (1965) p. 237-247.

Mayo Men who Died whilst Serving with the Connaught Rangers 1914-1918
Cathair Na Mart Vol. 7. (1) (1987) p. 21-31.

Newport Area Families 1864-1880
William G. Masterson (Indianapolis 1994)

Original Documents Relating to the Butler Lordship of Achill, Burrishoole and Aughrim
1236-1640. Galway Arch. and Hist. Soc. Jnl Vol. 15 (1933) p. 121-8

Quaker Weavers at Newport 1720-40
Friends Hist. Soc. Journal (1976)

The Compossicion Books of Conought
(transcribed by A. Martin Freeman (I.M.C. 1936)
Index of persons and place names to above (I.M.C. 1942)

The General Impact of the Encumbered Estates. Act of 1849 on Galway and Mayo.
J. Galway Arch. & Hist. Soc. p. 32, 44-74 (1972-73) & 38, p. 45-58 (1981-82)

The Glory of the Cong
J.A. Fahy Cong (1960)

The History of Co. Mayo to the Close of the 16th Century Herbert Thomas Knox (Dublin 1908)

The Mayo Binghams
Theresa Bingham Daly (Pentland Press 1997)

The Mayo Evictions of 1860 (Patrick Lavelle and the War in Partry)
Gerard P. Morgan (1986)

The Tenants of Dooleeg, Parish of Crossmolina 1764.
North Mayo Hist. & Arch Soc.. Vol. 1 (1) (1982) p 74-75.

The Titanic (Addergoole Casualties)
J. Nth Mayo Hist.and Arch Soc. Vol. 3 (3) (1995/6) p. 80-81

The Townlands of Inishboffin (with map)
Irish Geography Vol. 3 (3) (1956) p. 123-137

Visitations of the Dioceses of Clonfert, Tuam and Kilmacdaugh c. 1565-67
Analecta Hibernica (26) (1970)

Yeomanry Corps of Connaught, 1803
Irish Sword Vol. 3 (12) (1958) p. 187-193

Beacan/Bekan - Portrait of an East Mayo Parish
by Dr. Michael Comer and Nollaig O'Muraile. (Ballinrobe 1986)

Notes on placenames in Brownes Map of Mayo, 1584
Jnl. Galway Arch. And History Society. Vol. 6 (1909-1911)

Where the Sun Sets, Ballycroy, Belmullet, Kilcommon and Kiltane
by Fr. Sean Noone (Ballina 1991)

An Gorta Mor in gCill a Laidhe. (The Great Famine in Killala) Patricia Fitzgerald & Olive Kennedy (1996)

Clewbay Boating Disaster
Cathair Na Mart Vol 6.(1) 1986 p.5-23

A Various Country - Essays in mayo, 1500-1900
ed. Raymond Gillespie and Gerard Moran (Foilseachain Naisiunta Teoranta, Westport 1987)

The Surnames of Addergoole
Jnl. Mayo Nth Heritage Centre (1997) p.2-17

Deelbasin - An Historical Survey, Crossmolina Hist. and Arch. Society (1990).

Achill's Past
by Noreen Anne Gannon (Mayo 1990)

Chapter 15 Useful Addresses

Dublin Addresses

General Register Office Joyce House 8-11 Lombard Street East Dublin 2	Registers of all births, deaths and marriages in Ireland. Research room available
National Archives of Ireland Bishop Street Dublin 8	Holdings include, 1901 & 1911 census returns, wills and administrations, Griffiths valuations, tithe applotments and official papers.
National Library of Ireland Kildare Street Dublin 2	RC Church records, Griffiths valuations, tithe applotments, newspapers, Land Commission index, directories and other publications i.e. journals etc.
Genealogical Office 2 Kildare Street Dublin 2	Part of NLI; Extensive collection of genealogical manuscripts.
Gilbert Library 138-142 Pearse Street Dublin 2	Mainly Dublin material, but also holds Griffiths Valuations, Tithe applotments, 1914-18 war memorials etc
Registry of Deeds Henrietta Street Dublin 1	Deeds registered from 1708, Grantors index, land indexes, memorials and abstracts. Entry fee charged.
Land Registry (Western Region) Setanta Centre, Dublin 2	Registration of land title since 1892, with relevant maps.
Valuation Office 6 Ely Place, Dublin 2	Valuation records (Griffith & after), and maps.
Royal Irish Academy 19 Dawson Street, Dublin 2	A large collection of manuscripts and publications
Trinity College Library College Green, Dublin 2	A large collection of manuscripts and publications.

Mayo Addresses

Office of Superintendent Registrar New Antrim Street Castlebar, Co. Mayo	Registers of births, marriages and death for the county of Mayo
Mayo County Library Library Headquarters Castlebar Co. Mayo	Holdings include: 1901 census returns of Mayo, Mayo newspapers, Griffiths valuations, Ordance Survey field name books, Mayo folklore collections.
Mayo Nth Family Hist. Res. Centre MNFHRC Enniscoe, Castlehill Ballina Co. Mayo	Research service using indexed database of RC, CoI, Presbyterian and Methodist church records, school registers. Some estate records. Annual journal published. Research fee charged.
South Mayo Family Hist. Research Centre SMFHRC Main Street, Ballinrobe Co. Mayo http://www.mayo-ireland.ie/roots.htm	Research service using indexed database of RC, C.O.I., & Presbyterian church records, Voters lists, school registers, 17thcentury sources. Annual journal published Research fee charged.
Westport Historical Society Clewbay Heritage Centre The Quay Westport, Co. Mayo	Small collection of church records, school registers, rent rolls and street directories. Publishes Journal: 'Cathair na Mart' Research fee charged.
Mayo North Hist. & Arch. Soc. Remins Ballina, Co. Mayo	Monthly meetings held. Journal: North Mayo Hist. Journal

Religious Societies/Archives

Representative Church Body Library Braemor Park Churchtown, Dublin 14	Church of Ireland baptism, marriage and burial registers, vestry records also held.
Presbyterian Historical Soc. of Ireland Church House, Fisherwick Place Belfast BT1 6DW N. Ireland	Small collections of church records for Mayo.
Methodist Church of Ireland Methodist Manse Ardaghowen, Co. Sligo	Extant records for Mayo held, queries only by post.

Other Addresses

Irish Manuscripts Commission (IMC) 73 Merrion Square Dublin 2	The Commission has published about 160 titles since its establishment in 1928.

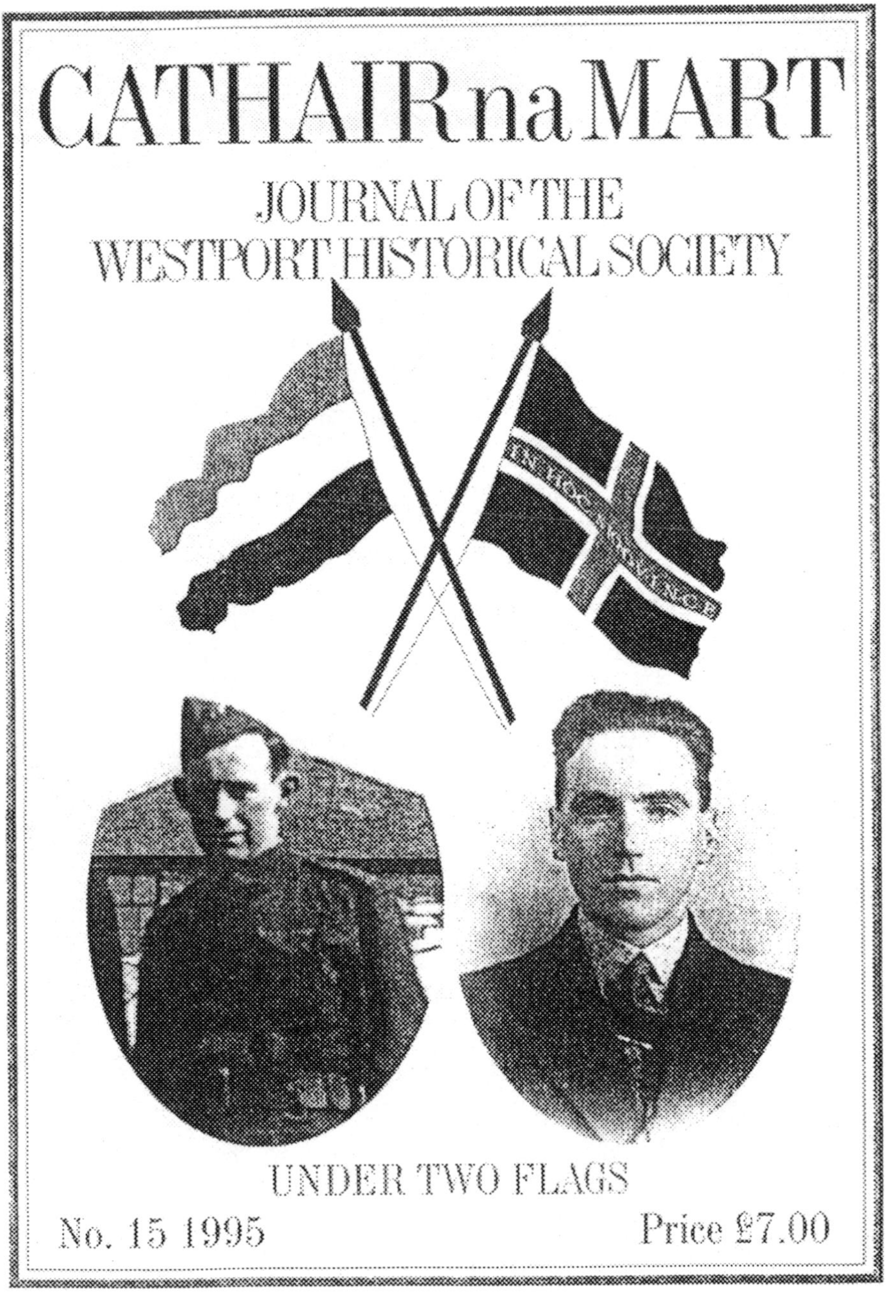

Cover of Cathair na Mart 1995

British Library, Newspaper Library Colindale Avenue Colindale, London NW7 5HE	Collection of Mayo newspapers in hard copy and on microfilm
Society of Genealogists 14 Charterhouse Buildings Goswell Road London EC1M 7BA	Library includes Irish section where directories, periodicals, indexes to various Irish records, some parish records and some newspapers are among its collection. Admission fee charged
Public Record Office of Nth Ireland 66 Balmoral Avenue Belfast BT9 6NY, N. Ireland	(PRONI) Holds a small collection of Mayo records
Andrew J. Morris PO Box 535 Farmington Michigan 48332, USA	Publisher of quarterly journal-'County Mayo Chronicles' and full name index to Griffiths Valuation of Co. Mayo.
Irish Genealogical Society, International P.O. Box 16585 St. Paul MN 55116-0585, USA	Quarterly Journal: 'The Septs.'; Library and other Irish research activities
Mayo Association New York 52-40, 39 Drive Woodside, New York 11377, USA	Association of Mayo people and descendants
Society of Australian Genealogists Richmond Villa 120 Kent Street Sydney NSW 2000	Extensive Library of Australia and Overseas Genealogical Reference Books; Quarterly Books; Quarterly Journal - 'Descent'
New Zealand Soc. Of Genealogists, Inc. P.O Box 8795 Auckland 3 New Zealand	Bi-Monthly Journal 'The New ZealandGenealogist'; meetings held at over 60 locations
Canadian Federation of Genealogical & Family History Societies 40 Celtic Bay Winnipeg Man. R3T 2W9 Canada	2 newsletters 'Canfed' published per year
Irish Military Research, Army, Navy, Aircorps. Joe White (former Irish Military Archives) e-mail: ASHLAWN@INDIGO.IE	Military Research for the period 1913-1966 only
Family History Centres (LDS) Finglas Road Dublin 9	Branch of Family History Library The Willows Salt Lake City, Utah, USA

THE

LANDOWNERS OF IRELAND.

An Alphabetical List

OF THE

OWNERS OF ESTATES

of 500 Acres or £500 Valuation and upwards,

IN IRELAND,

WITH

THE ACREAGE AND VALUATION IN EACH COUNTY.

AND ALSO CONTAINING

A BRIEF NOTICE OF THE EDUCATION AND OFFICIAL APPOINTMENTS OF EACH PERSON, TO WHICH ARE ADDED HIS TOWN AND COUNTRY ADDRESSES AND CLUBS.

COMPILED BY

U. H. HUSSEY DE BURGH,

Land Agent.

Dublin:

HODGES, FOSTER, AND FIGGIS,

GRAFTON STREET.

The front cover of 'The Landowners of Ireland'

CHAPTER XXXVII.

THE BARONY OF COSTELLO.

THIS barony is the lordship of MacCostello, from whom it takes its name, but was first named after Belahaunes. The part north of the parish of Aghamore was in the kingdom of Luighne or Gailenga, and was a subdivision of the latter called Sliabh Lugha. In St. Patrick's time the Ciarraige had some of the eastern part about Castlemore and the Letter, which they had lost by the thirteenth century.

As far back as history goes clearly, the southern part was in possession of the Ciarraige, successors of tribes called Cruithnech in the Attacottic list; but they make no great show in history, being one of the tribes on which Brian Orbsen's ancestors and descendants rested their supremacy in that early period when the legends give little more than names of chief kings.

In the thirteenth century it was held by two divisions called Ciarraige Uachtarach and Ciarraige Iochtarach, the latter better known as Ciarraige of Loch na nAirneadh, now Lough Mannin. O'Ceirin was chief of all, and had his principal dwelling on or near the lake. Mannin House is close to the site of Mannin Castle, which is on a small peninsula. The country about the lake is full of cashels and duns. In the lake were many crannoges. About the lake are many prehistoric graves and remains of cromlechs, evidence that for many ages the lake has been surrounded by the dwellings of families of high position.

In the de Burgo partition Hugh de Lacy had a grant of Sliabh Lugha. We next find Miles MacGoisdelbh established as lord of Sliabh Lugha. As he is said to have been married to a daughter of the Earl of Ulster, he probably got it from Hugh.

Jocelyn de Angulo came to Ireland with his sons Philip and Gilbert, called by the Irish MacGoisdelbh, where Goisdelbh is a corruption of Jocelyn, corrupted back into English as MacCostello. In Hugh de Lacy's enfeoffment of Meath, Jocelyn got the barony of the Navan, and his son Gilbert got Machaire Gaileng, comprising Morgallion and Ratoath. Philip and Gilbert were outlawed for rebellion in 1195. Gilbert's fiefs were forfeited, and were given by Walter de Lacy to his brother Hugh about 1198. In 1206 King John pardoned Philip and Gilbert and William de Angulo. This William had been

313

A page from H. Knox's 'History of Mayo'

Index

A
Aasleagh, 46
Abstracts of wills, 52, 55
ACHILL, 19, 20, 23, 37, 42, 46, 79, 81
Achonry, 41, 46, 52, 54, 56, 79
ADDERGOOLE, 20, 23, 42, 46, 70, 82
Administrations, 51
Administrative Divisions, 7, 15, 17
Aegis & Western Courier, 65
AGHAGOWER, 20, 23, 42, 46
AGHAMORE, 18, 20, 20, 23, 42, 46
Aghavower, 20
AGLISH, 20, 23, 42, 43, 46, 48, 50
ANNAGH, 20, 23, 42, 46, 69
Antrim, 31
ARDAGH, 20, 23, 42, 46
Ardnaree, 49
Armagh, 30, 31, 51, 56
Assizes, 31, 32, 34
Association for the Preservation of the Memorials of the Dead, 73
ATTYMASS, 20, 23, 32, 42, 46
Aughagower, 31
Aughaval, see Oughaval
Aughoose, 44

B
Backs, 42
Bal, 20
BALLA, 20, 23, 42, 46, 70, 73, 74, 75
Ballagh, 20
Ballina, 11, 27, 32, 36, 40, 49, 50, 52, 54, 63, 64, 65, 66, 67, 68, 70, 80, 84
Ballina Advertiser, 65
Ballina Chronicle, 65
Ballina Herald, 65
Ballina Impartial, 66
Ballina Journal & Connaught Advertiser, 66
Ballinamuck, 77
Ballinasmala, 73, 74
BALLINCHALLA, 20, 23, 42, 46, 49, 74
Ballincholla, 20
Ballindine, 36
BALLINROBE, 11, 20, 23, 27, 29, 30, 36, 42, 46, 63, 64, 66, 70, 73, 79, 80, 84
Ballinrobe Chronicle & Mayo Advertiser, 66
BALLINTOBER, 19, 20, 23, 42, 46
Ballycastle, 43, 48, 50, 74
Ballycroy, 44, 48, 80, 82
Ballyglass, 74
Ballyhane, 20
Ballyhaunis, 42, 64
BALLYHEAN, 19, 20, 23, 42, 48
BALLYNAHAGLISH, 20, 23, 32, 42,48
Ballynew, 36, 74
BALLYOVEY, 20, 23, 42, 48, 69, 74
BALLYSAKEERY, 20, 23, 42, 48, 50, 79, 80
Bangor, 44
Banns, 55, 56
Baptists, 41
Barony, 15
Barony Map, 24
Barrett, 69
Becan, 20
Begley, Donal F, 19
BEKAN, 20, 23, 43, 48, 82
Bellew, 70
Belmullet, 27, 44, 48, 82
Betham, William, 52
Bingham, 70, 81

Binghamstown, 49
Birth Records, 25
Blake, 71
BOHOLA, 20, 23, 43, 48, 69
Bourke, 80 see also Burke
Boyd, 70
Breaffy, 20, 70
BREAGHWY, 20, 23, 42, 43, 48
Breaghwee, 20
Brennan, 37, 69
Brewster, 70
British Army, 25, 34, 38, 81
British Library, 86
Browne, 36, 70, 71, 77, 80, 82
Browne Estate, 36
Bucholla, 20
Bull, Joseph, 77
Burial grounds, 73
Burial records, 46, 50
Burke, 69, 70
Burke Property, 38
BURRISCARRA, 20, 23, 42, 43, 48
BURRISHOOLE, 15, 20, 23, 31, 34, 43, 48, 50, 69, 74, 80, 81

C

Cancellation Books, 59
Carney, 37
Carra, 15, 34, 69, 71
Carracastle, 43
Carroll, 77
Castlebar, 11, 20, 27, 30, 42, 46, 50, 63, 64, 65, 66, 67, 70, 71, 73, 74, 77, 78, 84
CASTLEMORE, 20, 23, 43, 48, 69
Cathair na Mart, 30, 85
Catholic records, 41
Catholic Qualification Rolls, 30
Cavan, 31
Census - Irish Army, 39
Census of Ireland, 29, 33, 35, 37, 38
Census Search Applications, 38
Censuses, 17, 29
Chapel of Ease, 17
Chelsea Pensioners, 34
Church of Ireland, 9, 17, 39, 41, 46, 47, 50, 51, 73, 84
Church of Jesus Christ of Latter Day Saints, 27
Church Records, 41
Civil Divisions, 15
Civil Parish, 15
Civil Parish map, 24
Civil Registration, 25
Clanmorris, 15, 34, 36
Clare Island, 34, 36, 37, 44
Clare, Rev. Wallace, 55
Claremorris, 27, 43, 48, 63, 64, 70, 74, 79
Clarke, 37
Clew Bay Disaster, 37, 82
Clogher, 50
Cloonoghill, 45
Commercial & Social Directories, 63
CONG, 20, 23, 43, 48, 74, 79, 81
Congested Districts Board, 57, 61
Conlon, 37
Connaught, 11, 29, 65, 66, 67, 81, 82
Connaught Ranger, 32
Connaught Rangers, 81
Connaught Telegraph, 66
Connaught Watchman, 66
Consistorial court, 51
Convert Rolls, 39, 76
Coroners Inquests, 28
Costello, 15, 34, 36, 69, 71, 77, 81
CROSSBOYNE, 19, 20, 23, 36, 43, 48, 49, 70, 74
CROSSMOLINA, 11, 19, 20, 23, 34, 43, 48, 50, 79, 80, 82
Curry, 71

D

Daly, 71, 81
Death Records, 25, 41
Deceased Seamen, 27
Deeds, 59
DeMontmorency Estate, 36
Derry, 31
Dillon Estate, 31
Diocesan Administration Bond Indexes, 54
Diocesan court, 51, 52, 54
Diocesan Marriage Licences, 56
Directories, 39, 63
District Electoral Divisions, 17
District Registries, 52
Dolan, 70
DOONFEENY, 20, 23, 43, 48, 50, 74
Down, 31
DRUM, 20, 23, 42, 43, 48

Drummin, 45
Drummonahan, 20
Duffy, 12, 69
Dugort, 46
Dun Laoghaire, 37
Dunfeeny, 20
Durkan, 69

E
Ecclesiastical Courts, 52
Ecclesiastical Divisions, 17
Egan, 71
Elwood, 70
Emlafad, 49
Encumbered Estates, 57, 60, 81
Encumbered Estates Court, 57, 60
Ennisboffin, 20
Erris, 15, 43, 44, 50, 69, 80
Estate Records, 57, 61
Evictions, 37, 80, 81

F
Fair, 70
Family Histories, 69
Family History Centres, 27
Family Names, 69
Famine, 12, 82
Fermanagh, 31
Field Name Books, 18, 19, 61
First World War, 38
Fitzgerald, 70, 82
FlaxPremiums, 30
Foxford, 30, 32, 45, 49, 64
freeholders, 30, 32, 34
French invasion, 77

G
Gallagher, 12, 69
Gallen, 15, 34, 36, 38, 69
Galway, 48, 66, 70, 71
Galway etc Chronicle, 66
Galway Express, 66
Gaming Certificates, 34
Gaughan, 69
Genealogical Office, 9, 55, 83
Genealogical Publishing Co, 17
General Register Office, 25, 83
Gibbons, 69
Gilbert Library, 83
Gilgavower, 20
Glendenning, 71
Glynn, 71
Goblet, Yann, 17
Government Censuses, 29
Gravestone Inscriptions, 7, 73
Gray, 70
Greal, 71
Green Forms, 38
Griffiths Valuation, 31, 36,57, 58, 83
Gweesalia, 43

H
Heaney, 70
Heritage Centres, 12, 41
Higgins, 37, 71
Hollymount, 36, 50, 64, 74, 75, 77
Humbert, 77

I
Index to Births, 26
Inishboffin, 20
Innisboffin, 20
Innishark, 80
INNISHBOFFIN, 20, 23, 43, 48, 80, 82
International Genealogical Index, 27
Irish Army, 38, 39, 40
Irish Genealogical Society, 86
Irish Land Purchase & Settlement Co, 37
Irish Manuscripts Commission, 9, 19, 29, 84
Irish Memorials Association, 73
Irish War of Independence, 38
Irishman, 66
ISLANDEADY, 20, 23, 43, 48, 75
Islandedin, 20
Islandine

J
Jacobites, 30
Judge, 70

K
Keelogues, 44
Kelly, 5, 12, 37, 69, 70
KILBEAGH, 20, 23, 43, 48, 69
KILBELFAD, 20, 23, 43, 48, 71
Kilbreedy, 20
KILBRIDE, 20, 23, 43, 48

KILCOLMAN, 15, 19, 20, 23, 36, 43, 48, 74, 79
Kilcommin 20
KILCOMMON 15, 19, 20, 23, 43, 44, 48, 50, 69, 74, 75, 82
KILCONDUFF, 20, 23, 34, 44, 48, 69
KILCUMMIN, 20, 23, 34, 44, 48
KILDACAMMOGE, 20, 23, 44, 48
Kildavent, 37
Kildecamogue, 20
KILFIAN, 20, 23, 31, 41, 44, 48
Kilfraughans, 75
Kilfyan, 20
KILGARVAN, 20, 23, 32, 44, 48, 69
Kilgarvey, 20
KIlGEEVER, 19, 20, 23, 44, 49, 69, 75
KILLALA, 11, 19, 20, 23, 27, 31, 32, 41, 44, 46, 49, 50, 52, 54, 56, 63, 64, 74, 77, 78, 79, 81, 82
KILLASSER, 20, 23, 32, 41, 44, 49, 69, 81
KILLEDAN, 20, 23, 32, 44, 49, 69, 74, 75
Killedin, 20
KILMACLASSER, 20, 23, 44, 49
Kilmaine, 15, 34, 36, 44, 69, 74
KILMAINEBEG, 20, 23, 44, 49
KILMAINEMORE, 21, 23, 44, 49
KILMEENA, 21, 23, 44, 49, 75
Kilmina, 21
KILMOLARA, 21, 23, 74
KILMORE, 21, 23, 32, 44, 49, 69
KILMOREMOY, 21, 23
KILMOVEE, 21, 23, 45, 49, 69
Kilshalvey, 45
Kiltane, 43, 82
Kiltimagh, 37, 44
Kiltora, 21
KILTURRA, 21, 23, 45, 49
Kilturragh, 21
KILVINE, 21, 23, 45, 49
Kingstown, 37
Knappagh, 46
KNOCK, 21, 23, 31, 45, 49, 64
Knockdrumcalry, 21
Knockmore, 42

L

LACKAN, 19, 21, 23, 45, 49
Lambert, 70
Land Commission, 9, 55, 57, 60, 61
Land Records, 7, 31, 57
Land Registry, 57, 61, 83
Landed Estates Court, 60
Landholders, 32, 81
Lavelle, 81
leaseholders, 32
Lecanvey, 45
Lehinch, 36
Lewis's Topographical Dictionary, 19, 20
Linen Board Premiums, 30
Little, Rev. James, 77
Livingston, 70
Lodgers, 37
Lord Altamont, 30
Lord Clanmorris Estate, 34
Lord Sligo Estate, 31
Louisburgh, 44, 49
Lucan Estate, 80
Lynch, 71
Lyons, 6, 60, 69

M

MacDonald, 70
Magaunagh, 21
Mahon, 77
MANULLA, 19, 21, 23, 42, 45, 49
Manuscript Sources, 62
Maps, 24, 80, 82
Marquis of Sligo Estate, 31
Marriage Licence Bonds, 56
Marriage Licences, 7, 51, 54, 55, 56
Marriage Records, 25, 79
MAYO, 21, 45, 49
Mayo & Sligo Intelligencer, 67
Mayo 5000, 81
Mayo Abbey, 45, 74, 75, 81
Mayo Association New York, 86
Mayo burial grounds, 73
Mayo CoI Register, 49
Mayo Constitution, 66
Mayo County Council, 73
Mayo County Library, 84
Mayo Examiner, 67
Mayo Mercury & Connaught Advertiser, 67
Mayo News, 67
Mayo North Family History Res. Centre, 84
Mayo North Hist. & Arch. Soc, 84
Mayo Places, 79
Mayoman, 67

McCostello, 71
McDonald, 77
McDonnell, 69, 77
McGuire, 72
McHale, 69, 70
McNicholas, 69
McNulty, 69
MEELICK, 21, 23, 44, 45, 49
Mellett, 70
Methodist, 6, 41, 50, 73, 84
Migrants, 30, 31
Mill Books, 39
Millers, 39
Minola, 21
Monaghan, 31
Moore, 36, 70
Moore Hall Estate, 36
Moorgaga, 21
MOORGAGAGH, 21, 23, 45, 49
Moran, 12, 69, 82
Morris, 59, 70, 86
Moygawnagh, 49
MOYGOWNAGH, 21, 23, 31, 45
Moyne, 75
Mullaney, 72
Murphy, 69
Murrisk, 15, 34, 69, 74

N

Nally, 70, 79
National Archives of Ireland, 83
National Library, 6, 9, 27, 83
Neale, The, 43
Newport, 27, 43, 50, 63, 64, 74, 81
Newspapers, 65
Norman, 11, 12

O

O'Brien Rental Index, 60
O'Donel or O'Donnell, 69, 72, 80
O'Malley, 4, 12, 69, 70, 72, 80
Oath of allegiance, 30
Office of Superintendent Registrar, 27, 84
Old-age pension, 38 see also Pensions
Ordnance Survey, 18, 19, 80
Ormsby, 70
OUGHAVAL, 21, 23, 31, 45, 46, 47, 49, 50, 56, 69, 73, 74, 75

P

Parliamentary Gazetteer of Ireland, 19
Partry, 42, 74, 81
Pedigrees, 52, 70
Pensioners, 34
Pensions, 34, 38, 39, 40
Petty Sessions, 32
Petty's Mss Barony Maps, 17
Phillips, 72
PHSI, 50, 84
PHSI Library, 36, 84
Planters, 29
Police, 39
Poor Law Union, 15
Poor relief, 32
Post Office records, 30
Prendergast, 37
Prerogative Administration Grant Books, 52
Prerogative court, 51
Prerogative Court of Canterbury, 52
Prerogative Grant Indexes, 54
Prerogative marriage licences, 56
Prerogative Will Books, 52
Prerogative Will Indexes, 52
Prerogative Wills, 52, 53
Presbyterian, 6, 9, 36, 41, 50, 73, 84
Presbyterian Church Records, 50
Presbyterian Historical Soc. of Ireland, 36, 50, 84
Primary Sources, 13
Principal Registry, 52, 54
Probate, 51
Probate district, 54
Protestants, 30, 32
Public Record Office, 6, 10, 29, 46, 51, 86
Public Record Office of N. Ireland, 86

Q

Quaker, 81
Quit Rent, 30

R

Railway, 80
Rathduff, 42
Rathrea, 21
RATHREAGH, 21, 23, 45, 49
Rebellion of 1641, 29
Rebellion of 1798, 31, 77

Registry of Deeds, 54, 57, 59, 83
Representative Church Body Library, 10, 46, 84
Research on Mayo families, 12
ROBEEN, 21, 23, 44, 45, 49
Roman Catholic, 41
ROSSLEE, 21, 23, 42, 45, 49
Roundfort, 44
Royal Irish Academy, 29, 83
Royal Irish Constabulary, 39
Ruane, 69
Ruttledge, 70

S
Salmon, 37
Schools, 36, 39, 40
Seamen, 27
Secondary Sources, 13
Shareholders, 37
Shipwrecks, 79
Shraigh, 39
Shruel, 21
SHRULE, 21, 23, 41, 45, 49, 71
Sligo, 31, 49, 50, 65, 66, 67, 68, 71, 84
Society of Genealogists, 86
South Mayo Family History Research Centre, 84
Srade, 21
Sraide, 21
St. Muirdeacha's College, 40
Stafford Inquisition, 29
Stock, Dr. Joseph, 77
Strade, 21
Sraide, 21
Surnames, 7, 52, 79, 82
Swineford, 27
Swinford, 27, 63, 64

T
TAGHEEN, 21, 23, 36, 43, 45, 49
Taghkeen, 21
Taugheen, 21
Telegraph, 32, 34, 66, 67
TEMPLEMORE, 21, 23, 32, 45, 49
TEMPLEMURRY, 21, 23, 45, 49
Testamentary Card Index, 54
The Neale, 43
Tighe, 70
Titanic, 82
Tithe Applotments, 31, 32, 34, 57
Tithepayers, 31, 32, 34
TOOMORE, 21, 23, 45, 49
TOUAGHTY, 21, 23, 45, 49
Tourmakeady, 42
Towaghty, 21, 23
Towmore, 21
townland, 15
Townland Index of Ireland, 17
Traders, 32
Transplantation, 29
Treston, 70
Trinity College, 83
Tuam, 41, 46, 52, 54, 56, 79, 82
TURLOUGH, 19, 21, 23, 45, 49, 50, 69, 74, 80
Tuymore, 21
Tyrawley, 15, 36, 66, 69
Tyrawly Herald, 67
Tyrone, 31

U
Ulster Immigrants, 11, 31
Urlare Abbey, 74

V
Valuation Office, 59, 83
Vicar's, 53
Voters List, 32, 36, 39, 84

W
Walsh, 12, 37, 69
War Memorials, 38
Weavers, 81
Wesleyan Methodist, 50
Western Gem, 67
Western Nationalist, 68
Western People, 65, 68
Western Star, 68
Westport, 6, 11, 27, 30, 31, 32, 37, 45, 49, 50, 63, 64, 67, 70, 74, 77, 84, 85
Westport Historical Society, 84
William III., 30
Wills, 51

Y
Yearly Calendars - Wills, 55
Yeomanry Corps, 82

Index to Illustrations

Sample page from 'General Alphabetical Index of Townlands & Towns, Parishes & Baronies of Ireland' 16

Sample page from Ordnance Survey Field Name Book for the Civil Parish of Aghamore 18

Description of Aghamore from the Topographical Dictionary of Ireland by Samuel Lewis 24

Civil parishes in alphabetical order 20/21

Map of Civil Parishes of Mayo 23

Sample page from Index to Births Registered in Ireland in 1865 26

1901 Census Return from the townland of Corhawnagh, Aghamore 33

1911 Census Return from the townland of Corhawnagh, Aghamore 35

Church of Ireland Baptismal Register of Oughaval, Co. Mayo (1865) 47

Sample page from Sir Arthur Vicar's Index to Prerogative Wills of Ireland 1536-1810 53

Extract from Griffith's Primary Valuation of Ireland 58

Extract from Hayes' 'Manuscript Sources for the History of Irish Civilisation' 62

Extract from 'J. Association for Preservation of the Memorials of the Dead' 75

Sample page from 'The Convert Rolls' by Eileen O'Byrne 76

Page from 'The Last Invasion of Ireland' by Richard Hayes 78

Sample cover of 'Cathair na Mart' 85

The front cover of 'The Landowners of Ireland' 87

A page from H. Knox's 'History of Mayo' 88